English
Essentials

Differentiated Comprehension for SATs

John O'Connor &
Roy Blatchford

Student's Book

LONGMAN

CONTENTS

Page

4   Introduction
5   Reading Performance Grid: National Curriculum & Key Stage 3 SATs

	Grammar Spelling Punctuation	Contents of Homework File
Section 1: Fiction		
6 **The Book of the Banshee** *Anne Fine*	capital letters	1 The Book of the Banshee *(earlier extract)*
10 **The Ratcatcher** *Roald Dahl*	full stops & commas	2 The Ratcatcher *(earlier extract)*
15 **Harry Potter &** **the Philosopher's Stone** *JK Rowling*	the subject of the sentence	3 Harry Potter & the Philosopher's Stone *(earlier extract)*
19 **The Conjuror's Revenge** *Stephen Leacock*	question marks & exclamation marks	4 The Conjurer's Revenge *(same extract + exercises)*
23 ***Three Men in a Boat** *Jerome K Jerome*	dialect	5 Three Men in a Boat *(later extract)*
27 **I Used To Live Here Once** *Jean Rhys*	verbs	6 The Fisherman *Jonas Lie*
30 ***The Signal-man** *Charles Dickens*	punctuation of dialogue	7 The Signal-man *(end of story)*
34 **Examination Day** *Henry Sleasar*	adverbs	8 Fahrenheit 451 *Ray Bradbury*
39 ***Great Expectations** *Charles Dickens*	reported speech	9 Great Expectations *(extract continued)*
43 ***Kidnapped** *Robert Louis Stevenson*	figurative language	10 Kidnapped *(extract continued)*
47 **The Flowers** *Alice Walker*	nouns & adjectives	11 The Flowers *(story extract + exercises)*
50 **Five Hours to Simla** *Anita Desai*	apostrophes for possession	12 The God of Small Things *Arundhati Roy*
Section 2: Drama		
54 **The Thwarting of Baron Bolligrew** *Robert Bolt*	concrete nouns & proper nouns	13 Maid Marian and her Merry Men *BBC Television*
58 ***Frankenstein** *Mary Shelley* *(adapted by Philip Pullman)*	abstract nouns	14 Frankenstein *(extract continued)*
62 **Red Dwarf: Psirens** *Rob Grant & Doug Naylor*	revising adjectives	15 Red Dwarf *(extract continued)*
66 ***Silas Marner** *George Eliot* *(adapted by John O'Connor)*	revising verbs	16 Silas Marner *(original novel)*

Page		Grammar Spelling Punctuation	Contents of Homework File	
70	The Computer Nut *Betsy Byars* *(adapted by Marcy Kahan)*	simple sentences	17	The Computer Nut *(same extract + exercises)*
74	*Androcles and the Lion *Bernard Shaw*	apostrophes for abbreviation	18	Androcles and the Lion *(extract continued)*
78	Fawlty Towers: Basil the Rat *John Cleese & Connie Booth*	standard English	19	Fawlty Towers: Basil the Rat *(extract continued)*
83	Journey's End *RC Sherriff*	the changing language	20	Journey's End *(extract continued)*

Section 3: Poetry

Page		Grammar Spelling Punctuation	Contents of Homework File	
87	*The Pied Piper of Hamelin *Robert Browning*	revising apostrophes	21	The Pied Piper of Hamelin *(later extract)*
92	'Poem for My Sister' & 'Sisters' *Liz Lochhead & Wendy Cope*	hyphens & dashes	22	For Heidi with Blue Hair *Fleur Adcock*
95	'A Case of Murder' & 'The Secret in the Cat' *Vernon Scannell & May Swenson*	revising figurative language	23	The Daydreamer *Ian McEwan*
99	'Catching Crabs' & 'Praise Song for My Mother' *David Dabydeen & Grace Nichols*	revising dialect	24	Granny in de Market Place *Amryl Johnson*
102	*The Charge of the Light Brigade *Alfred Lord Tennyson*	prepositions	25	'Dulce et Decorum Est' & 'Mental Cases' *Wilfred Owen*
105	'A Crabbit Old Woman' & 'For My Grandmother Knitting' *Phyllis McCormack & Liz Lochhead*	poetry & prose	26	'Look Closer' & 'A Nurse's Reply' *Phyllis McCormack & Liz Hogben*
110	'Hurricane' & 'Wind' *James Berry & Ted Hughes*	verb tenses	27	'Hurricane' & 'Wind' *(same poems + exercises)*
113	*If *Rudyard Kipling*	revising abstract nouns	28	Hamlet *William Shakespeare*

Section 4: Non-fiction

Page		Grammar Spelling Punctuation	Contents of Homework File	
116	The Warrington Bombings *Keith Greenberg*	revising capital letters	29	The Warrington Bombings *(extract continued)*
119	A Chance in Six Million *Marianne Elsley*	revising commas	30	A Chance in Six Million *(extract continued)*
123	Hieroglyphs *Tobias Chapman*	'h' in spelling	31	Hints on Pronunciation for Foreigners *The Sunday Times*
127	The Fate of the Turkey *Edward Pilkington*	clauses	32	Bad Tidings for the Pets from *The Guardian*
131	*Nursing in the Great War *Eleonora B Pemberton*	wh- clauses	33	Letters *Florence Nightingale*
134	Comics & Science *Rob McKay & Paul Phillips*	brackets & dashes	34	Frankenstein *Mary Shelley*
138	Letter to Daniel *Fergal Keane*	paragraphs	35	Notes from a Small Island *Bill Bryson*
142	*The Great Fire of London *Samuel Pepys*	the changing language	36	The Great Fire of London *(later extract)*

* pre 20th-century writing

INTRODUCTION

Step-by-step to a better SATs grade!

Reading is much more enjoyable if you are good at it. *English Essentials* is for people who need more experience in reading, as well as for those who are successful readers and who really enjoy it.

This book will give you the right kind of practice to gain your best possible results in the SATs: your English tests in Year 9.

How to use this book

The four sections: These are devoted to the four main kinds of writing – Fiction, Poetry, Drama and Non-Fiction.

The units: Each unit has a **text**, such as a short story, a complete poem, or sometimes an extract. Each text starts with **learning objectives** that make sure you understand which reading skills you need to practise in order to answer the questions.

Four kinds of questions are included for **differentiation**:

- **'Checking the facts' questions** ask the most important details. Brief answers are needed for these.
- **'A' questions** ask you to retell the main details, or to describe things from the text. Fuller answers are needed.
- **'B' questions** ask for more explanation – more 'reading between the lines' – or they ask you to compare things from the text.
- **'C' questions** ask for very full answers, requiring you to look closely at the language in the text and analyse things in detail, sometimes expressing your personal opinion.

The grid on the next page shows how these **differentiated** questions match the National Curriculum Level Descriptions for Reading, and the QCA Performance Criteria. These are used to mark your work in the SATs.

The Homework File has photocopiable homework sheets for each unit in this book. They follow up your classwork, and build on what has been learned. SATs tests with sample answers are also included to give you practice with real past papers.

Reading Comprehension Performance Grid:
The National Curriculum & Key Stage 3 SATs

This grid will help you understand the types of answers you need to aim for in order to improve your reading comprehension skills and SATs grades.

Type of question given in this book	Type & level of answer expected in the SATs	National Curriculum Level Description	Typical QCA Performance Criteria for SATs
A WRITE ABOUT	Mainly retelling and describing.	**Level 4:** ...pupils show an understanding of significant ideas, themes, events and characters... They refer to the text when explaining their views. They locate and use ideas and information.	**Level 4:** Pupils make simple references although they may tend to repeat or paraphrase what is in the passage... Even though they narrate, their selection of facts is generally relevant... They make simple inferences...
		Lower Level 5: Pupils show understanding of a range of texts, selecting essential points...	**Lower Level 5:** Pupils give an explanation which shows some understanding, even though answers lack detail... and answers may not be always closely linked to the text...
B COMMENT UPON	More 'reading between the lines'; comparisons; some reference to language, structure and themes.	**Upper Level 5:** Pupils use inference and deduction where appropriate... They identify key features, themes and characters, and select sentences, phrases and relevant information to support their views. They retrieve and collate information from a range of sources.	**Upper Level 5:** Pupils select one or two words and phrases from the text to support their ideas... They show an overall understanding... and comment briefly on the importance of references made...
		Level 6: Pupils identify different layers of meaning and comment on their significance and effect. They give personal responses, referring to language, structure and themes in justifying their views...	**Level 6:** Pupils give some comment on implicit ideas... Some points are supported by appropriate reference to the text... or developed in detail. There is some awareness of the writer's use of language...
C Discuss	Full, perceptive answers which analyse the text closely.	**Level 7:** Pupils show understanding of the ways in which meaning and information are conveyed... They articulate personal and critical responses... showing awareness of their thematic, structural and linguistic features. They select and synthesise a range of information...	**Level 7:** Pupils give a reasonably full answer, which includes a discussion of the writer's use of language, and recognises how the writer conveys ideas... Views are supported by well-explained textual references...
		Above level 7: Pupils... evaluate how authors achieve their effects through the use of linguistic, structural and presentational devices. They select and analyse information and ideas...	**Above level 7:** Pupils give full and perceptive answers which analyse the text... There is evidence of a personal response which is rooted in the text and they use references skilfully to justify their comments...

THE BOOK OF THE BANSHEE

FROM A NOVEL BY ANNE FINE

Learning objectives

- to understand how a writer establishes themes at the start of a novel
- to understand how a writer creates humour

Discussion

- What are the ingredients of an enjoyable and successful lesson in school?
- What skills do the best teachers have?

THE STORY SO FAR

The central character and narrator of the novel is Will Flowers. He is a keen reader and is particularly excited when he and his friend Chopper meet a visiting author in the school reception. Then, unexpectedly, she sweeps into their classroom to talk about her work …

'My name's Alicia Whitley.'

That, in itself, caught most people's attention. We spend whole periods pestering the staff to tell us their first names. When you hear someone her age just stand up and announce theirs, you take a bit of interest.

'I'm a writer,' she went on. 'That's how I earn my living and I'm going to talk to you about writing books.'

Chopper let out a groan. It was only a little one, a tiny one really. But she still heard it at the front.

She stopped dead.

'Chopper!' she ordered. 'Come down and sit here.'

She pointed to the row of empty seats at the front.

Chopper was astonished. So was everyone else (including Mr Astley). I knew already just how quick she was with names, and she'd heard Chopper's, of course, when Scotbags bellowed at him. But as I've already mentioned, Chopper's not bright, and in the shock of the moment he forgot that.

He stood up, beet-red and nervous.

'Chum me!' he whispered, desperate.

So I stood up, too, and together we threaded our way to the front between the chairs she'd just shoved out in careless wavy rows. Mr Astley stirred in his seat. I thought for a moment he was about to speak up and send me back. You know the sort of thing. 'Excuse me! I don't believe I heard anybody mentioning *your* name ...' But it was as if Alicia Whitley saw it coming, and once again she seemed quite amiably to wave him aside.

'I'll let Will come with you, Chopper, just so long as you both listen.'

There was an unmistakable notch-up of tension. You could tell what they were all thinking: 'Does this woman know *everyone's* name?' And then they all settled down.

Chopper sprawled on his new chair, sunk in the deepest despair. And I – I stared at Alicia Whitley.

I was all ears.

I don't know what it was that interested me so much. Part of it might have been that she talked so fast. She talked a blue streak, at about a hundred miles an hour, and that made it feel as if it wasn't just another boring lesson.

She talked fast, but she never said the same thing twice, so if you weren't paying attention – bad luck, *poof!* you missed it. She talked so fast you practically had to sit up straight to hear. She pulled one thing after another out of the bag to show us. Mucky scribbled sheets of paper with huge crossings-out that she said were the first go at the first pages, written at top speed, just to get into it.

She showed us pages written a bit more neatly, later, with grubby patches where she'd rubbed out over and over again to try things around different ways. On some of the sheets she'd rubbed things out so often she had giant holes in the paper.

'April,' she said.

She kept talking, all about how she kept at it, day after day, week after week, month after month. Then she showed us pages she'd typed up, all smart and clean.

'September,' she said.

I thought we must be pretty well through by now. But, no. Almost at once she held up a matching typed sheet, but this one was covered with pencilled corrections and crossings-out and additions. She'd clearly been at it all over again.

'October,' she told us. 'But we are getting there.'

November was pretty neat. It was all typed out beautifully, and it was only because I was in the front row that I could see little splodges on the paper where the light hit the back and showed she'd been using her Tippex.

Then, suddenly, she swooped in the bag again and pulled out a large green file. On the front was a label that said in big letters: *The Rise and Hard Fall of Stewart Moffat.*

'December!' she said triumphantly.

'Alec Whitsun!' I said, astonished.

It just came out. I couldn't help it.

She stared at me. First she looked pleased, then anxious. She broke off talking to everybody for a second, and dipping in front of me, her skirts brushing the floor, she asked:

'You don't mind?'

'Oh, no,' I said. I was really embarrassed now. 'Not at all.' And just as she rose to her full height, I added stupidly: 'Sorry.'

I knew exactly what she meant, though, when she asked 'Do you mind?' She was worried in case it would spoil the books for me, knowing they'd been written by an Alicia, not an Alec. I've read all ten Whitsun books. I think they're brilliant. For years I thought that there were only four. Then one day, purely by accident, I found another, and in the front of that there was a list – 'Other Books by Alec Whitsun' – with six more titles I had never seen, including *The Rise and Hard Fall of Stewart Moffat.* It took me ages to get hold of all of them because the Alec Whitsuns were the sort of books people grab straight off the library trolley and don't put down in case someone else makes off with them. It was so odd to think he was standing there – *she* was standing there – holding a file of pages that she'd written over and over, and then typed, and I'd read through school and supper and late into the night, with all my pillows pushed up against the bottom of the door, to stop Mum and Dad from noticing I hadn't put my light out.

'Questions?' she said suddenly.

Questions

Checking the facts

❶ Why does Will comment on the fact that Alicia Whitley uses her first name in front of the class?

❷ How does Chopper react when Alicia Whitley says that she is going to talk to the class about writing books?

❸ How does Alicia Whitley quickly establish her authority with the class?

❹ Why does the writer plan her talk around the months of the year?

❺ What is the link between Alicia Whitley and Alec Whitsun?

 A *What picture do you have of Alicia Whitley?*

WRITE ABOUT

- her appearance
- her actions
- the way she responds to pupils
- her interest in her own work.

 B *Will Flowers's passion for reading is an important part of the novel. How does the author highlight Will's enjoyment of words and books?*

COMMENT UPON

- how Will reacts and speaks to Alicia Whitley
- his interest in her writing process
- his reading passions.

 C *How does the author make her writing lively and vivid?*

DISCUSS

- her descriptions of pupils
- the way she caricatures teachers
- her use of short sentences and dialogue
- her use of the first-person narrator.

Grammar Spelling Punctuation

Capital letters

Make a list of 25 words from the extract which begin with a capital letter.

- Now sort them into lists, according to *why* each word begins with a capital letter. For example: 'Because it is at the beginning of a sentence …'.

Writing

'The Classroom Visitor' – write your own story with this title.

- Try to create a scene in which normal classroom life is strangely and comically disturbed by the visitor. You might begin: 'As soon as s/he walked in I knew that …'

THE RATCATCHER

F R O M   A   S H O R T   S T O R Y   B Y   **R O A L D   D A H L**

Learning objectives

- to understand how a writer uses language to create suspense

- to understand how a short story writer makes every word count

Discussion

- Have you ever witnessed something which was both amazing and revolting at the same time? What happened that meant you just couldn't look away? Describe the scene or event.

THE STORY SO FAR

The narrator and his friend Claud have called the ratcatcher to their farm because they have rat infestation. The ratcatcher is keen to show off just how well he understands rats …

'You want to see somethin' you'd never even *believe* unless you seen it with your own eyes?' the ratman asked.

I glanced at Claud, slightly apprehensive. 'Yes,' Claud said.

'Come on then, let's see.'

The ratman slipped the dead rat back into one pocket, the ferret into the other. Then he reached down into his knapsack and produced – if you please – a second live rat.

'Good Christ!' Claud said.

'Always got one or two rats about me somewhere,' the man announced calmly. 'You got to know rats on this job, and if you want to know 'em you got to have 'em round you. This is a sewer rat, this is. An old sewer rat, clever as buggery. See him watchin' me all the time, wonderin' what I'm goin' to do? See him?'

'Very unpleasant.'

'What are you going to do?' I asked. I had a feeling I was going to like this one even less than the last.

'Fetch me a piece of string.'

Claud fetched him a piece of string.

With his left hand, the man looped the string around one of the rat's hind legs. The rat struggled, trying to turn its head to see what was going on, but he held it tight around the neck with finger and thumb.

'Now!' he said, looking about him. 'You got a table inside?'

'We don't want the rat inside the house,' I said.

'Well – I need a table. Or somethin' flat like a table.'

'What about the bonnet of that car?' Claud said.

We walked over to the car and the man put the old sewer rat on the bonnet. He attached the string to the windshield wiper so that the rat was now tethered.

At first it crouched, unmoving and suspicious, a big-bodied grey rat with bright black eyes and a scaly tail that lay in a long curl upon the car's bonnet. It was looking away from the ratman, but watching him sideways to see what he was going to do. The man stepped back a few paces and immediately the rat relaxed. It sat up on its haunches and began to lick the grey fur on its chest. Then it scratched its muzzle with both front paws. It seemed quite unconcerned about the three men standing near by.

'Now – how about a little bet?' the ratman asked.

'We don't bet,' I said.

'Just for fun. It's more fun if you bet.'

'What d'you want to bet on?'

'I'll bet you I can kill that rat without usin' my hands. I'll put my hands in my pockets and not use 'em.'

'You'll kick it with your feet,' Claud said.

It was apparent that the ratman was out to earn some money. I looked at the rat that was going to be killed and began to feel slightly sick, not so much because it was going to be killed but because it was going to be killed in a special way, with a considerable degree of relish.

'No,' the ratman said. 'No feet.'

'Nor arms?' Claud asked.

'Nor arms. Nor legs, nor hands neither.'

'You'll sit on it.'

'No. No squashin'.'

'Let's see you do it.'

'You bet me first. Bet me a quid.'

'Don't be so bloody daft,' Claud said. 'Why should we give you a quid?'

'What'll you bet?'

'Nothin'.'

'All right. Then it's no go.'

He made as if to untie the string from the windshield wiper.

'I'll bet you a shilling,' Claud told him. The sick gastric sensation in my stomach was increasing, but there was an awful magnetism about this business and I found myself quite unable to walk away or even move.

'You too?'

'No,' I said.

'What's the matter with you?' the ratman asked.

'I just don't want to bet you, that's all.'

'So you want me to do this for a lousy shillin'?'

'I don't want you to do it.'

'Where's the money?' he said to Claud.

Claud put a shilling piece on the bonnet, near the radiator. The ratman produced two sixpences and laid them beside Claud's money. As he stretched out his hand to do this, the rat cringed, drawing its head back and flattening itself against the bonnet.

'Bet's on,' the ratman said.

Claud and I stepped back a few paces. The ratman stepped forward. He put his hands in his pockets and inclined his body from the waist so that his face was on a level with the rat, about three feet away.

His eyes caught the eyes of the rat and held them. The rat was crouching, very tense, sensing extreme danger, but not yet frightened. The way it crouched, it seemed to me it was preparing to spring forward at the man's face; but there must have been some power in the ratman's eyes that prevented it from doing this, and subdued it, and then gradually frightened it so that it began to back away, dragging its body backwards with slow crouching steps until the string tautened on its hind leg. It tried to struggle back further against the string, jerking its leg to free it. The man leaned forward towards the rat, following it with his face, watching it all the time with his eyes, and suddenly the rat panicked and leaped sideways in the air. The string pulled it up with a jerk that must almost have dislocated its leg.

It crouched again, in the middle of the bonnet, as far away as the string would allow, and it was properly frightened now, whiskers quivering, the long grey body tense with fear.

At this point, the ratman again began to move his face closer. Very slowly he did it, so slowly there wasn't really any movement to be seen at all except that the face just happened to be a fraction closer each time you looked. He never took his eyes from the rat. The tension was considerable and I wanted suddenly to cry out and tell him to stop. I wanted him to stop because it was making me feel sick inside, but I couldn't bring myself to say the word. Something extremely unpleasant was about to happen – I was sure of that. Something sinister and cruel and ratlike, and perhaps it really would make me sick. But I had to see it now.

The ratman's face was about eighteen inches from the rat. Twelve inches. Then ten, or perhaps it was eight, and then there was not more than the length of a man's hand separating their faces. The rat was pressing its body flat against the car bonnet, tense and terrified. The ratman was also tense, but with a dangerous active tensity that was like a tight-wound spring. The shadow of a smile flickered around the skin of his mouth.

Then suddenly he struck.

He struck as a snake strikes, darting his head forward with one swift knifelike stroke that originated in the muscles of the lower body, and I had a momentary glimpse of his mouth opening very wide and two yellow teeth and the whole face contorted by the effort of mouth-opening.

More than that I did not care to see. I closed my eyes, and when I opened them again the rat was dead and the ratman was slipping the money into his pocket and spitting to clear his mouth.

'That's what they make lickerish out of,' he said. 'Rat's blood is what the big factories and the chocolate-people use to make lickerish.'

Again the relish, the wet-lipped, lip-smacking relish as he spoke the words, the throaty richness of his voice and the thick syrupy way he pronounced the word *lickerish*.

'Don't talk so absolutely disgusting,' Claud told him.

'Ah! but that's it, you see. You eaten it many a time. Penny sticks and lickerish bootlaces is all made from rat's blood. Boiled up, it is, in great cauldrons, bubblin' and steamin' and men stirrin' it with long poles.

Suddenly he noticed that his audience was no longer with him, that our faces were hostile and sick-looking and crimson with anger and disgust. He stopped abruptly, and without another word he turned and sloped off down the driveway out on to the road, moving with the slow, that almost delicate ambling walk that was like a rat prowling, making no noise with his footsteps even on the gravel of the driveway.

Questions

Checking the facts

❶ How is the narrator feeling when the ratcatcher first asks him if wants to see something amazing?

❷ Why does the ratcatcher want his audience to place a bet?

❸ Why does the narrator find himself unable to look away from what is going on with the rat?

❹ Why does the ratcatcher smile just before he finally pounces on the rat?

❺ Why does the ratcatcher end up talking about 'lickerish'?

A   *What picture do you have of the ratcatcher?*

WRITE ABOUT
- his conversation
- his preparations for killing the rat
- his plan of attack
- his comments after the death of the rat.

 B   *What emotions do Claud and the narrator experience during the course of this episode?*

COMMENT UPON
- their inner thoughts
- their words to each other
- their words to the ratcatcher
- their actions.

 C   *How does Roald Dahl build up this scene to be one in which the reader feels s/he must read on to see what happens next?*

DISCUSS
- the way the three characters interact
- the unfolding of the action, and the way it is structured
- the author's use of dialogue
- the vocabulary; the length of sentences and paragraphs; the final paragraph.

Grammar Spelling Punctuation

Full stops and commas

Reread lines 16 to 33, p.12 ('Claud and I ...' to '... with fear').
In order to create drama and suspense, how does the writer use:

- the comma?
- the full-stop?

- Now write your own paragraph of about ten lines in which you describe a tense situation. Use these three forms of punctuation to good effect!

Writing

Write your own short story titled 'The Bet'.
- Aim to set up 'the bet' in the first part of your story – and then to keep your reader guessing right to the very end of the tale.

HARRY POTTER AND THE PHILOSOPHER'S STONE

FROM A NOVEL BY J K ROWLING

Learning objectives

- to understand how a writer has the reader laughing at and with her characters
- to understand how a writer establishes character in the early pages of a novel

Discussion

- Do you believe that some people have 'special powers' of one kind or another? For example, can they really see into the future or the past?

THE STORY SO FAR

The Dursley family are proud to say they used to be a perfectly normal family.... until their nephew Harry Potter – with his strange, magical powers – came to live with them. Dudley Dursley's birthday treat is a family outing to the zoo, with best friend Piers …

It was a very sunny Saturday and the zoo was crowded with families. The Dursleys bought Dudley and Piers large chocolate ice-creams at the entrance and then, because the smiling lady in the van had asked Harry what he wanted before they could hurry him away, they bought him a cheap lemon ice lolly. It wasn't bad either, Harry thought, licking it as they watched a gorilla scratching its head and looking remarkably like Dudley, except that it wasn't blond.

Harry had the best morning he'd had in a long time. He was careful to walk a little way apart from the Dursleys so that Dudley and Piers, who were starting to get bored with the animals by lunch-time, wouldn't fall back on their favourite hobby of hitting him. They ate in the zoo restaurant and when Dudley had a tantrum because his knickerbocker glory wasn't big enough, Uncle Vernon bought him another one and Harry was allowed to finish the first.

Harry felt, afterwards, that he should have known it was all too good to last.

After lunch they went to the reptile house. It was cool and dark in here, with lit windows all along the walls. Behind the glass, all sorts of lizards and snakes were crawling and slithering over bits of wood and stone. Dudley and Piers wanted to see huge, poisonous cobras and thick, man-crushing pythons. Dudley quickly found the largest snake in the place. It could have wrapped its body twice around Uncle Vernon's car and crushed it into a dustbin – but at the moment it didn't look in the mood. In fact, it was fast asleep.

Dudley stood with his nose pressed against the glass, staring at the glistening brown coils.

'Make it move,' he whined at his father. Uncle Vernon tapped on the glass, but the snake didn't budge.

'Do it again,' Dudley ordered. Uncle Vernon rapped the glass smartly with his knuckles, but the snake just snoozed on.

'This is boring,' Dudley moaned. He shuffled away.

Harry moved in front of the tank and looked intently at the snake. He wouldn't have been surprised if it had died of boredom itself – no company except stupid people drumming their fingers on the glass trying to disturb it all day long. It was worse than having a cupboard as a bedroom, where the only visitor was Aunt Petunia hammering on the door to wake you up, at least he got to visit the rest of the house.

The snake suddenly opened its beady eyes. Slowly, very slowly, it raised its head until its eyes were on a level with Harry's.

It winked.

Harry stared. Then he looked quickly around to see if anyone was watching. They weren't. He looked back at the snake and winked too.

The snake jerked its head towards Uncle Vernon and Dudley, then raised its eyes to the ceiling. It gave Harry a look that said quite plainly:

'I get that all the time.'

'I know,' Harry murmured through the glass, though he wasn't sure the snake could hear him. 'It must be really annoying.'

The snake nodded vigorously.

'Where do you come from, anyway?' Harry asked.

The snake jabbed its tail at a little sign next to the glass. Harry peered at it.

Boa Constrictor, Brazil.

'Was it nice there?'

The boa constrictor jabbed its tail at the sign again and Harry read on: *This specimen was bred in the zoo.* 'Oh, I see – so you've never been to Brazil?'

As the snake shook its head, a deafening shout behind Harry made both of them jump: 'DUDLEY! MR DURSLEY! COME AND LOOK AT THIS SNAKE! YOU WON'T *BELIEVE* WHAT IT'S DOING!'

Dudley came waddling towards them as fast as he could.

'Out of the way, you,' he said, punching Harry in the ribs. Caught by surprise, Harry fell hard on the concrete floor. What came next happened so fast no one saw how it happened – one second, Piers and Dudley were leaning right up close to the glass, the next, they had leapt back with howls of horror.

Harry sat up and gasped; the glass front of the boa constrictor's tank had vanished. The great snake was uncoiling itself rapidly, slithering out on to the floor – people throughout the reptile house screamed and started running for the exits.

As the snake slid swiftly past him, Harry could have sworn a low, hissing voice said: 'Brazil, here I come … Thanksss, amigo.'

The keeper of the reptile house was in shock.

'But the glass,' he kept saying, 'where did the glass go?'

The zoo director himself made Aunt Petunia a cup of strong sweet tea while he apologised over and over again. Piers and Dudley could only gibber. As far as Harry had seen, the snake hadn't done anything except snap playfully at their heels as it passed, but by the time they were all back in Uncle Vernon's car, Dudley was telling them how it had nearly bitten off his leg, while Piers was swearing it had tried to squeeze him to death. But worst of all, for Harry at least, was Piers calming down enough to say: 'Harry was talking to it, weren't you, Harry?'

Uncle Vernon waited until Piers was safely out of the house before starting on Harry. He was so angry he could hardly speak. He managed to say, 'Go – cupboard – stay – no meals,' before he collapsed into a chair and Aunt Petunia had to run and get him a large brandy.

Harry lay in his dark cupboard much later, wishing he had a watch. He didn't know what time it was and he couldn't be sure the Dursleys were asleep yet. Until they were, he couldn't risk sneaking to the kitchen for some food.

Questions

Checking the facts

❶ How does the writer tell us that Dudley and cousin Harry don't like each other?

❷ How might we guess that Dudley is a rather moody, spoilt child?

❸ Why does Harry sympathise with the snake in the reptile house?

❹ What part does Piers play in the drama that follows?

How do we know that Harry Potter is not well treated by the Dursley family?

WRITE ABOUT
- the attitude towards him of Dudley and Piers
- the words and actions of Uncle Vernon
- the words and actions of Aunt Petunia
- his bedroom and home-life.

 How does the author create comedy in the scene in the reptile house?

COMMENT UPON
- the description of the lizards and snakes
- the eye contact and 'conversations' between the snake and Harry
- the disappearance of the tank's glass front
- the family reactions to the episode.

 Show how, although the author writes in the third person, we always see the events through Harry's eyes.

DISCUSS
- Harry's impressions of the gorilla (paragraph 1)
- the feeling expressed in paragraph 3
- the comparison between the snake's boredom and Harry's
- the way the writer relates Harry's conversation with the snake
- the final paragraph.

Grammar Spelling Punctuation

The subject of the sentence

Reread the first four paragraphs from this extract, up to line 7, p.16 ('fast asleep').

- Now write out any five sentences from these paragraphs, and underline the words or words which make up the *subject* of that sentence.

- Compare your work with another student's. What is a useful definition for the *subject* of a sentence? Do all sentences have to have a subject?

Writing

Harry Potter actually turns out to be a wizard! Write another episode in the life of Harry Potter, in which his magic powers play havoc with Dursley family life.

- Aim for about 350 words. This could be in story or script form.

THE CONJURER'S REVENGE

A SHORT STORY BY STEPHEN LEACOCK

Learning objectives

- to understand how a short story is constructed to keep readers guessing
- to understand how a writer uses language to create comedy and irony

Discussion

- Think of a time when someone has tried to embarrass you in front of others. How did you feel? Did you think about how you might get your own back?

'Now, ladies and gentlemen,' said the conjurer, 'having shown you that the cloth is absolutely empty, I will proceed to take from it a bowl of goldfish. Presto!'

All around the hall people were saying, 'Oh, how wonderful! How does he do it?'

But the Quick Man on the front seat said in a big whisper to the people near him, 'He – had – it – up – his – sleeve.'

Then the people nodded brightly at the Quick Man and said, 'Oh, of course', and everybody whispered round the hall, 'He – had – it – up – his – sleeve.'

'My next trick,' said the conjurer, 'is the famous Hindustani rings. You will notice that the rings are apparently separate; at a blow they all join (clang, clang, clang) – Presto!'

There was a general buzz of stupefaction till the Quick Man was heard to whisper, He – must – have – had – another – lot – up – his – sleeve.'

Again everybody nodded and whispered, 'The – rings – were – up – his – sleeve.'

The brow of the conjurer was clouded with a gathering frown.

'I will now,' he continued, 'show you a most amusing trick by which I am enabled to take any number of eggs from a hat. Will some gentleman kindly lend me his hat? Ah, thank you – Presto!'

He extracted seventeen eggs, and for thirty-five seconds the audience began to think that he was wonderful. Then the Quick Man whispered along the front bench, 'He – has – a – hen – up – his – sleeve,' and all the people whispered it on. 'He – has – a – lot – of – hens – up – his – sleeve.'

The egg trick was ruined.

It went on like that all through. It transpired from the whispers of the Quick Man that the conjurer must have concealed up his sleeve, in addition to the rings, hens and fish, several packs of cards, a loaf of bread, a doll's cradle, a live guinea-pig, a fifty-cent piece, and a rocking-chair.

The reputation of the conjurer was rapidly sinking below zero. At the close of the evening he rallied for a final effort.

'Ladies and gentlemen,' he said, 'I will present to you, in conclusion, the famous Japanese trick recently invented by the natives of Tipperary. Will you, sir,' he continued, turning toward the Quick Man, 'will you kindly hand me your gold watch?'

It was passed to him.

'Have I your permission to put it into this mortar and pound it to pieces?' he asked savagely.

The Quick Man nodded and smiled.

The conjurer threw the watch into the mortar and grasped a sledge hammer from the table. There was a sound of violent smashing, 'He's – slipped – it – up – his – sleeve,' whispered the Quick Man.

'Now, sir,' continued the conjurer, 'will you allow me to take your handkerchief and punch holes in it? Thank you. You see, ladies and

gentlemen, there is no deception; the holes are visible to the eye.'

The face of the Quick Man beamed. This time the real mystery of the thing fascinated him.

'And now, sir, will you kindly pass me your silk hat and allow me to dance on it? Thank you.'

The conjurer made a few rapid passes with his feet and exhibited the hat crushed beyond recognition.

'And will you now, sir, take off your celluloid collar and permit me to burn it in the candle? Thank you, sir. And will you allow me to smash your spectacles for you with my hammer? Thank you.'

By this time the features of the Quick Man were assuming a puzzled expression. 'This thing beats me,' he whispered, 'I don't see through it a bit.'

There was a great hush upon the audience. Then the conjurer drew himself up to his full height and, with a withering look at the Quick Man he concluded:

'Ladies and gentlemen, you will observe that I have, with this gentleman's permission, broken his watch, burnt his collar, smashed his spectacles, and danced on his hat. If he will give me the further permission to paint green stripes on his overcoat, or to tie his suspenders in a knot, I shall be delighted to entertain you. If not, the performance is at an end.'

And amid a glorious burst of music from the orchestra the curtain fell, and the audience dispersed, convinced that there are some tricks, at any rate, that are not done up the conjurer's sleeve.

Questions

Checking the facts

The conjurer

❶ How many tricks does he perform up to line 9, p.20?

❷ How many tricks does he perform with the Quick Man's belongings?

The Quick Man

❸ How many times does he try to ruin the conjurer's performance?

❹ Which of his personal belongings does the Quick Man give to the conjurer?

How does the Quick Man try to turn the audience against the conjurer?

WRITE ABOUT

- the Quick Man's actions
- the words and phrases he uses
- the way he speaks
- the way the audience reacts.

 In what ways does the conjurer plan and carry out his revenge?

COMMENT UPON

- his words to the audience
- the tricks he performs
- the reactions of the Quick Man
- the conclusion to the performance.

 How does Stephen Leacock build the humour and tension in this short story?

DISCUSS

- the changing feelings of both the conjurer and the Quick Man
- the structure of the story
- the use of dialogue and of narrative description
- the ironies of the final three paragraphs (4 lines from the bottom onwards, p.20).

Grammar Spelling Punctuation

Question marks and exclamation marks

At the beginning of this story, the conjurer's sentences are either statements (ending in full stops) or exclamations (ending in exclamation marks).

- Find one example of each in the final speech.

- At what point in the story does the conjurer ask his first question? List all his questions and discuss in pairs why the conjurer switches over from statements to questions.

Writing

Write your own short story (300–400 words) in which one character 'turns the tables' on another.

The story could be:

- based on an actual event you have seen or been part of
- completely imaginary
- comic or serious or a mixture of both.

THREE MEN IN A BOAT

FROM A NOVEL BY JEROME K JEROME

Learning objectives

- to understand how comic writing is presented by a pre-1900 author

- to understand how a writer makes every word count and keeps his readers guessing

Discussion

- Is it possible to tell a story without 'telling lies'? In other words, whenever someone retells a story, do they exaggerate a little? Can you think of an example when you've done this for a particular reason – perhaps to help someone or to save embarrassing a friend?

THE STORY SO FAR

Three young men and their dog are taking a rowing holiday on the River Thames. One evening, they find themselves in a riverside pub enjoying a drink, and they start talking to an old man …

Then a pause ensued in the conversation, during which our eyes wandered round the room. They finally rested upon a dusty old glass-case, fixed very high up above the chimney-piece, and containing a trout. It rather fascinated me, that trout; it was such a monstrous fish. In fact, at first glance, I thought it was a cod.

'Ah!' said the old gentleman, following the direction of my gaze, 'fine fellow that, ain't he?'

'Quite uncommon,' I murmured; and George asked the old man how much he thought it weighed.

'Eighteen pounds six ounces,' said our friend, rising and taking down his coat. 'Yes,' he continued, 'it wur sixteen year ago, come the third o' next month, that I landed him. I caught him just below the bridge with a minnow. They told me he wur in the river, and I said I'd have him, and so I did. You don't see many fish that size about here now, I'm thinking. Good night, gentlemen, good night.'

And out he went, and left us alone.

We could not take our eyes off the fish after that. It really was a remarkably fine fish. We were still looking at it, when the local carrier, who had just stopped at the inn, came to the door of the room with a pot of beer in his hand, and he also looked at the fish.

'Good-sized trout, that,' said George, turning round to him.

'Ah! You may well say that, sir,' replied the man; and then, after a pull at his beer, he added, 'Maybe you wasn't here, sir, when that fish was caught?'

'No,' we told him. We were strangers in the neighbourhood.

'Ah!' said the carrier, 'then, of course, how should you? It was nearly five years ago that I caught that trout.'

'Oh! Was it you who caught it, then?' said I.

'Yes, sir,' replied the genial old fellow. 'I caught him just below the lock – leastways, what was the lock then – one Friday afternoon; and the remarkable thing about it is that I caught him with a fly. I'd gone out pike fishing, bless you, never thinking of a trout, and when I saw that whopper on the end of my line, blest if it didn't quite take me aback. Well, you see, he weighed twenty-six pound. Good night, gentlemen, good night.'

Five minutes afterwards a third man came in, and described how *he* had caught it early one morning, with bleak; and then he left, and a stolid, solemn-looking, middle-aged individual came in, and sat down over by the window.

None of us spoke for a while; but, at length, George turned to the newcomer, and said:

'I beg your pardon, I hope you will forgive the liberty that we – perfect strangers in the neighbourhood – are taking, but my friend here and myself would be so much obliged if you would tell us how you caught that trout up there.'

'Why, who told you I caught that trout!' was the surprised query.

We said that nobody had told us so, but somehow or other we felt instinctively that it was he who had done it.

'Well, it's a most remarkable thing – most remarkable,' answered the stolid stranger, laughing; 'because, as a matter of fact, you are quite right. I did catch it. But fancy your guessing it like that. Dear me, it's really a most remarkable thing.'

And then he went on, and told us how it had taken him half an hour to land it, and how it had broken his rod. He said he had weighed it carefully when he reached home, and it had turned the scale at thirty-four pounds.

He went in his turn, and when he was gone, the landlord came in to us. We told him the various histories we had heard about his trout, and he was immensely amused, and we all laughed very heartily.

'Fancy Jim Bates and Joe Muggles and Mr Jones and old Billy Maunders all telling you that they had caught it. Ha! ha! ha! Well, that is good,' said the honest old fellow, laughing heartily. 'Yes, they are the sort to give it *me*, to put up in *my* parlour, if *they* had caught it, they are! Ha! ha! ha!'

And then he told us the real history of the fish. It seemed that he had caught it himself, years ago, when he was quite a lad.

He was called out of the room at this point, and George and I turned our gaze upon the fish.

It really was a most astonishing trout. The more we looked at it, the more we marvelled at it. It excited George so much that he climbed up on the back of a chair to get a better view of it.

And then the chair slipped, and George clutched wildly at the trout-case to save himself, and down it came with a crash, George and the chair on top of it.

'You haven't injured the fish, have you?' I cried in alarm, rushing up.

'I hope not,' said George, rising cautiously and looking about.

But he had. That trout lay shattered into a thousand fragments – I say a thousand, but they may have only been nine hundred. I did not count them.

We thought it strange and unaccountable that a stuffed trout should break up into little pieces like that.

And so it would have been strange and unaccountable, if it had been a stuffed trout, but it was not.

The trout was plaster of Paris.

Questions

Checking the facts

❶ The men say that they are 'strangers in the neighbourhood'. Why is this detail important?

❷ What different bait is said to have been used to catch the fish?

❸ How many men claim to have caught the fish?

❹ What different claims are made for the weight of the fish?

❺ What is 'plaster of Paris'?

Describe in your own words the comings and goings of the evening in the pub.

WRITE ABOUT

- the strangers
- the locals
- the fishy tales they tell
- the final moments.

 What ingredients in the stories make them seem truthful or exaggerated?

COMMENT UPON

- the way each person falls into conversation with the strangers
- how and where the fish is caught
- the weight of the fish
- whether you think the strangers are being deliberately tricked.

 How does the author make this scene funny and how does he involve his readers?

DISCUSS

- how George and the narrator lead events
- the use of dialogue and the repetition of certain phrases
- the careful choice of vocabulary
- the length of paragraphs; the build-up to the story's climax
- how you respond to the story.

Grammar Spelling Punctuation

Dialect

The author features local Oxfordshire dialect in parts of the story.

- Make a list of the words and phrases which are used, for example: 'fine fellow that, ain't he?'. Rewrite in standard English the examples you've selected.

- Which words and phrases used by the 'strangers' mark them out as visitors to the area? Describe their use of language.

Writing

Write an account of a 'famous sporting victory' you've taken part in – and present an exaggerated story of your part or a friend's part in that victory.

I USED TO LIVE HERE ONCE

A SHORT STORY BY JEAN RHYS

She was standing by the river looking at the stepping stones and remembering each one. There was the round unsteady stone, the pointed one, the flat one in the middle – the safe stone where you could stand and look around. The next wasn't so safe for when the river was full the water flowed over it and even when it showed dry it was slippery. But after that it was easy and soon she was standing on the other side.

The road was much wider than it used to be but the work had been done carelessly. The felled trees had not been cleared away and the bushes looked trampled. Yet it was the same road and she walked along feeling extraordinarily happy.

It was a fine day, a blue day. The only thing was that the sky had a glassy look that she didn't remember. That was the only word she could think of. Glassy. She turned the corner, saw that what had been the old pavé[1] had been taken up, and there too the road was much wider, but it had the same unfinished look.

[1] Stone cobbled road

She came to the worn stone steps that led up to the house and her heart began to beat. The screw pine was gone, so was the mock summer house called the ajoupa, but the clove tree was still there and at the top of the steps the rough lawn stretched away, just as she remembered it. She stopped and looked towards the house that had been added to and painted white. It was strange to see a car standing in front of it.

There were two children under the big mango tree, a boy and a little girl, and she waved to them and called 'Hello' but they didn't answer her or turn their heads. Very fair children, as Europeans born in the West Indies so often are: as if the white blood is asserting itself against all odds.

The grass was yellow in the hot sunlight as she walked towards them. When she was quite close she called again, shyly: 'Hello'. Then, ' I used to live here once,' she said.

Still they didn't answer. When she said for the third time 'Hello' she was quite near them. Her arms went out instinctively with the longing to touch them.

It was the boy who turned. His grey eyes looked straight into hers. His expression didn't change. He said 'Hasn't it gone cold all of a sudden. D'you notice? Let's go in.'

'Yes let's,' said the girl.

Her arms fell to her sides as she watched them running across the grass to the house. That was the first time she knew.

Questions

Checking the facts

❶ How many stepping stones are described?

❷ How is the main character feeling?

❸ Which country is the story set in?

❹ How many times does the woman try to speak to the children?

❺ What do you understand by the last line?

What are the key points in this story?

WRITE ABOUT

- the woman approaching the house
- the woman speaking to the children
- the words and actions of the children.

 Describe the setting for this story.

COMMENT UPON

- the climate
- the river
- the road
- the house.

 What ingredients of a ghost story does 'I Used To Live Here Once' have?

DISCUSS

- the descriptions of place
- the description of the woman and children meeting
- clues about the woman's identity
- key words and phrases in the story.

Grammar Spelling Punctuation

Verbs

The use of verbs – dynamic and stative – is important in this story.

- Draw up two columns, headed DYNAMIC and STATIVE. List seven verbs in each column.

- What 'actions' are important in this story? What 'thoughts' are important?

Writing

Write your own ghost story in which it is not clear until the end of the story that one of the characters *is* in fact a ghost.

- Aim for about 350–400 words.

THE SIGNAL-MAN

FROM A SHORT STORY BY
CHARLES DICKENS

Learning objectives

- to understand how a short-story writer makes the narrator a character in the story

- to understand how a writer creates atmosphere

Discussion

- What makes a good ghost story? Pick the best ghost story that you know and discuss what makes it successful.

THE STORY SO FAR

Walking in the countryside, the narrator comes across a lonely signal-box at the bottom of a gloomy ravine where the railway line emerges from a tunnel. The signal-man seems frightened about something and admits that he had at first mistaken his visitor for someone else he once saw there ... 'A man who looks like me?', asks the visitor ...

'I don't know. I never saw the face. The left arm is across the face, and the right arm is waved – violently waved. This way.'

I followed his action with my eyes, and it was the action of an arm gesticulating[1], with the utmost passion and vehemence, 'for God's sake, clear the way!'

'One moonlight night,' said the man, 'I was sitting here, when I heard a voice cry, "Halloa! Below there!" I started up, looked from that door, and saw this. Someone else standing by the red light near the tunnel, waving as I just now showed you. The voice seemed hoarse with shouting, and it cried, "Look out! Look out!" and then again, "Halloa! Below there! Look out!" I caught up my lamp, turned it on red, and ran towards the figure, calling, "What's wrong? What has happened? Where?" It stood just outside the blackness of the tunnel. I advanced so close upon it that I wondered at its keeping the sleeve across its eyes. I ran right up at it and had my hand stretched out to pull the sleeve away, when it was gone.'

[1] His arm made desperate and urgent movements

'Into the tunnel?' said I.

'No. I ran on into the tunnel, five hundred yards. I stopped, and held my lamp above my head, and saw the figures of the measured distance, and saw the wet stains stealing down the walls and trickling through the arch. I ran out again faster than I had run in (for I had a mortal abhorrence of the place upon me), and I looked all round the red light with my own red light, and I went up the iron ladder to the gallery atop of it, and I came down again, and ran back here. I telegraphed both ways, "An alarm has been given. Is anything wrong?" The answer came back, both ways, "All well." '

Resisting the slow touch of a frozen finger tracing out my spine, I showed him how this figure must be a deception of his sense of sight …

'As to an imaginary cry,' said I, 'do but listen for a moment to the wind in this unnatural valley while we speak so low, and to the wild harp it makes of the telegraph wires.'

That was all very well, he returned, after we had sat listening for a while, and he ought to know something of the wind and the wires, – he who so often passed long winter nights there, alone and watching. But he would beg to remark that he had not finished.

I asked his pardon, and he slowly added these words, touching my arm, – 'Within six hours after the Appearance, the memorable accident on this Line happened, and within ten hours the dead and wounded were brought along through the tunnel over the spot where the figure had stood.'

A disagreeable shudder crept over me, but I did my best against it. It was not to be denied, I rejoined, that this was a remarkable coincidence, calculated deeply to impress his mind.

'This,' he said, again laying his hand upon my arm, and glancing over his shoulder with hollow eyes, 'was just a year ago. Six or seven months passed, and I had recovered from the surprise and shock, when one morning, as the day was breaking, I, standing at the door, looked towards the red light and saw the spectre again.' He stopped with a fixed look at me.

'Did it cry out?'

'No. It was silent.'

'Did it wave its arm?'

'No. It leaned against the shaft of the light, with both hands before the face. Like this.'

Once more I followed his action with my eyes. It was an action of mourning. I have seen such an attitude in stone figures on tombs.

'Did you go up to it?'

'I came in and sat down, partly to collect my thoughts, partly because it had turned me faint. When I went to the door again, daylight was above me, and the ghost was gone.'

'But nothing followed? Nothing came of this?'

He touched me on the arm with his forefinger twice or thrice, giving a ghastly nod each time:

'That very day, as a train came out of the tunnel, I noticed, at a carriage window on my side, what looked like a confusion of hands and heads, and something waved. I saw it just in time to signal the driver, Stop! He shut off, and put his brake on, but the train drifted past here a hundred and fifty yards or more. I ran after it, and, as I went along, heard terrible screams and cries. A beautiful young lady had died instantaneously in one of the compartments, and was brought in here, and laid down on this floor between us.'

Involuntarily I pushed my chair back, as I looked from the boards at which he pointed to himself.

'True, sir. True. Precisely as it happened, so I tell it to you.'

I could think of nothing to say to any purpose, and my mouth went dry. The wind and the wires took up the story with a long lamenting wail.

Questions

Checking the facts

❶ What does the signal-man say is troubling him at the beginning of this extract?

❷ What was the spectre doing when the signal-man first saw it? What did it shout out?

❸ What incident took place six hours after the first appearance of the spectre?

❹ How long was it after the first appearance of the spectre that the signal-man saw it for a second time?

❺ What was it doing then?

A

What stories does the signal-man tell the visitor about the two appearances of the spectre?

WRITE ABOUT

- what the spectre seemed to be doing when the signal-man first saw him
- the accident that took place on the line shortly afterwards
- the appearance of the spectre when the signal-man saw it for the second time
- the event that followed.

What picture do you form of the narrator of the story?

COMMENT UPON

- his reaction to the signal-man's story about the spectre's first appearance and the first accident on the line
- the way he listens to the signal-man and encourages him to speak
- his detailed attention to the signal-man's behaviour
- his reactions to the story of the spectre's second appearance and the death which followed.

How does Dickens create an atmosphere of fear and foreboding in this extract?

DISCUSS

- the signal-man's expressions of fear and his behaviour as he tells each part of the story
- the narrator's changing attitudes to the various developments in the tale
- the details of the setting and the atmosphere created for each of the spectre's appearances.

Grammar Spelling Punctuation

Punctuation of dialogue

A great deal of this story is told through dialogue. In pairs, look back at the opening ten lines of the extract and find examples of the following rules:

- speech marks placed around the words a person actually says
- a new speaker's words placed on a different line, as though starting a new paragraph
- spoken words started with a capital letter
- the punctuation mark (for example: comma, question mark, exclamation mark or full stop) placed at the end of the speech, inside the speech marks.

Writing

Write the first 250 words of a ghost or mystery story which is set in a remote or gloomy setting.

- You could write in the first person ('I slowly descended the cliff …') or the third person ('She looked about her …'). Find a good setting such as a lighthouse, a deserted airfield or ruined castle.

EXAMINATION DAY

A SHORT STORY BY **HENRY SLEASAR**

Learning objectives

- to understand how a short story is crafted
- to understand how a writer builds suspense through narrative

Discussion

- What is the purpose of examinations in school? Do you think they help children to learn and teachers to teach?

The Jordans never spoke of the exam, not until their son, Dickie, was 12 years old. It was on his birthday that Mrs Jordan first mentioned the subject in his presence, and the anxious manner of her speech caused her husband to answer sharply.

'Forget about it,' he said. 'He'll do all right.'

They were at the breakfast table, and the boy looked up from his plate curiously. He was an alert-eyed youngster, with flat blond hair and a quick, nervous manner. He didn't understand what the sudden tension was about, but he did know that today was his birthday, and he wanted harmony above all. Somewhere in the little apartment there were wrapped, be-ribboned packages waiting to be opened, and in the tiny wall-kitchen, something warm and sweet was being prepared in the automatic stove. He wanted the day to be happy, and the moistness of his mother's eyes, the scowl on his father's face, spoiled the mood of fluttering expectation with which he had greeted the morning.

'What exam?' he asked.

His mother looked at the tablecloth. 'It's just a sort of Government intelligence test they give children at the age of 12. You'll be taking it next week. It's nothing to worry about.'

'You mean a test like in school?'

'Something like that,' his father said, getting up from the table. 'Go and read your comics, Dickie.' The boy rose and wandered towards that part of the living room which had been 'his' corner since infancy. He fingered the topmost comic of the stack, but seemed uninterested in the colourful squares of fast-paced action. He wandered towards the window, and peered gloomily at the veil of mist that shrouded the glass.

'Why did it have to rain today?' he said. 'Why couldn't it rain tomorrow?'

His father, now slumped into an armchair with the Government newspaper, rattled the sheets in vexation. 'Because it just did, that's all. Rain makes the grass grow.'

'Why, Dad?'

'Because it does, that's all.'

Dickie puckered his brow. 'What makes it green, though? The grass?'

'Nobody knows,' his father snapped, then immediately regretted his abruptness.

Later in the day, it was birthday time again. His mother beamed as she handed over the gaily-coloured packages, and even his father managed a grin and a rumple-of-the-hair. He kissed his mother and shook hands gravely with his father. Then the birthday cake was brought forth, and the ceremonies concluded.

An hour later, seated by the window he watched the sun force its way between the clouds.

'Dad' he said, 'how far away is the sun?'

'Five thousand miles,' his father said.

Dickie sat at the breakfast table and again saw moisture in his mother's eyes. He didn't connect her tears with the exam until his father suddenly brought the subject to light again.

'Well, Dickie,' he said, with a manly frown. 'You've got an appointment today.'

'I know Dad. I hope –'

'Now, it's nothing to worry about. Thousands of children take this test every day. The Government wants to know how smart you are, Dickie. That's all there is to it.'

'I get good marks in school,' he said hesitantly.

'This is different. This is a – special kind of test. They give you this stuff to drink, you see, and then you go into a room where there's a sort of machine –'

'What stuff to drink?' Dickie said.

'It's nothing. It tastes like peppermint. It's just to make sure you answer the questions truthfully. Not that the Government thinks you won't tell the truth, but this stuff makes *sure*.'

Dickie's face showed puzzlement, and a touch of fright. He looked at his mother, and she composed her face into a misty smile.

'Everything will be all right,' she said.

'Of course it will,' his father agreed. 'You're a good boy, Dickie; you'll make out fine. Then we'll come home and celebrate. All right?'

'Yes, sir,' Dickie said.

They entered the Government Educational Building fifteen minutes before the appointed hour. They crossed the marble floors of the great pillared lobby, passed beneath an archway and entered an automatic lift that brought them to the fourth floor.

There was a young man wearing an insignia-less tunic, seated at a polished desk in front of Room 404. He held a clipboard in his hand, and he checked the list down to the Js and permitted the Jordans to enter.

The room was as cold and official as a courtroom, with long benches flanking metal tables. There were several fathers and sons already there, and a thin-lipped woman with cropped black hair was passing out sheets of paper.

Mr Jordan filled out the form, and returned it to the clerk. Then he told Dickie: 'It won't be long now. When they call your name, you just go through the doorway at that end of the room.' He indicated the portal with his finger.

A concealed loudspeaker crackled and called off the first name. Dickie saw a boy leave his father's side reluctantly and walk slowly towards the door.

At five minutes to eleven, they called the name of Jordan.

'Good luck, son,' his father said, without looking at him. 'I'll call for you when the test is over.'

Dickie walked to the door and turned the knob. The room inside was dim, and he could barely make out the features of the grey-tunicked attendant who greeted him.

'Sit down,' the man said softly. He indicated a high stool beside his desk. 'Your name's Richard Jordan?'

'Yes, sir.'

'Your classification number is 600–115. Drink this, Richard.'

He lifted a plastic cup from the desk and handed it to the boy. The liquid inside had the consistency of buttermilk, tasted only vaguely of the promised peppermint. Dickie downed it, and handed the man the empty cup.

He sat in silence, feeling drowsy, while the man wrote busily on a sheet of paper. Then the attendant looked at his watch, and rose to stand only inches from Dickie's face. He unclipped a penlike object from the pocket of his tunic, and flashed a tiny light into the boy's eyes.

'All right,' he said. 'Come with me, Richard.'

He led Dickie to the end of the room, where a single wooden armchair faced a multi-dialled computing machine. There was a microphone on the left arm of the chair, and when the boy sat down, he found its pinpoint head conveniently at his mouth.

'Now just relax, Richard. You'll be asked some questions, and you think them over carefully. Then give your answers into the microphone. The machine will take care of the rest.'

'Yes, sir.'

'I'll leave you alone now. Whenever you want to start, just say "ready" into the microphone.'

'Yes, sir.'

The man squeezed his shoulder, and left.

Dickie said, 'Ready.'

Lights appeared on the machine, and a mechanism whirred. A voice said; 'Complete this sequence. One, four, seven, ten ...'

Mr and Mrs Jordan were in the living room, not speaking, not even speculating.

It was almost four o'clock when the telephone rang. The woman tried to reach it first, but her husband was quicker.

'Mr Jordan?'

The voice was clipped; a brisk, official voice.

'Yes, speaking.'

This is the Government Educational Service. Your son, Richard M. Jordan, Classification 600–115, has completed the Government examination. We regret to inform you that his intelligence quotient is above the Government regulation, according to Rule 84, Section 5, of the New Code.'

Across the room, the woman cried out, knowing nothing except the emotion she read on her husband's face.

'You may specify by telephone,' the voice droned on, 'whether you wish his body interred by the Government, or would you prefer a private burial place? The fee for Government burial is ten dollars.'

Questions

Checking the facts

❶ What is Mr Jordan's state of mind in the early part of the story?

❷ How is Mrs Jordan feeling?

❸ How do you know this story is set at some time in the future?

❹ Why is everyone handed a liquid to drink before the test?

❺ What is the purpose of the examination?

What picture do you have of Mr and Mrs Jordan throughout this story?

WRITE ABOUT

- their inner thoughts and feelings
- their actions
- how they speak to one another
- how they speak to Dickie.

 How does Dickie approach the examination?

COMMENT UPON

- his thoughts and actions over breakfast
- the questions he asks his parents
- his observations on the Government Educational Building
- how he responds during the test.

 What view of a future world is the author trying to project in this story?

DISCUSS

- the setting for the narrative
- how the people of this time live their lives
- the actions of 'The Government'
- how the story ends.

Grammar Spelling Punctuation

Adverbs

Find the following adverbs from the short story:

sharply	immediately	suddenly	manly	hesitantly
truthfully	reluctantly	busily	conveniently	

- What does each adverb add to the phrase where it is being used?
  Think of an alternative adverb that the writer could have used.
  For example:
     'caused her husband to answer sharply'
     'caused her husband to answer *firmly*'.

- Now write your own nine sentences, using one of the above adverbs in each sentence.

Writing

Write your own science fiction story, based around the idea of a Government controlling children's intelligence.

- Like all science fiction, try to make the plot both fantastical *and* believable!

GREAT EXPECTATIONS

FROM A NOVEL BY **CHARLES DICKENS**

Learning objectives

- to understand how a pre-1900 author involves his readers at the start of a novel

- to understand how a writer develops atmosphere and character through vivid vocabulary

Discussion

- Think of a time when you found yourself in a very scary situation. Looking back now, how much was real and how much was imagination?

THE STORY SO FAR

Pip, a young boy, has just entered the church graveyard where his parents and five brothers are buried …

Ours was the marsh country, down by the river, within, as the river wound, twenty miles of the sea. My first most vivid and broad impression of the identity of things, seems to me to have been gained on a memorable raw afternoon towards evening. At such a time I found out for certain that this bleak place overgrown with nettles was the churchyard; and that Philip Pirrip, late of this parish, and also Georgiana wife of the above, were dead and buried; and that Alexander, Bartholomew, Abraham, Tobias, and Roger, infant children of the aforesaid, were also dead and buried; and that the dark flat wilderness beyond the churchyard, intersected with dykes and mounds and gates, with scattered cattle feeding on it, was the marshes; and that the low leaden line beyond was the river; and that the distant savage lair from which the wind was rushing, was the sea; and that the small bundle of shivers growing afraid of it all and beginning to cry, was Pip.

'Hold your noise!' cried a terrible voice, as a man started up from among the graves at the side of the church porch. 'Keep still, you little devil, or I'll cut your throat!'

A fearful man, all in coarse grey, with a great iron on his leg. A man with no hat, and with broken shoes, and with an old rag tied round his head. A man who had been soaked in water, and smothered in mud, and lamed by stones, and cut by flints, and stung by nettles, and torn by briars; who limped and shivered, and glared and growled; and whose teeth chattered in his head as he seized me by the chin.

'O! Don't cut my throat, sir,' I pleaded in terror. 'Pray don't do it, sir.'
'Tell us your name!' said the man. 'Quick!'
'Pip, sir.'
'Once more,' said the man, staring at me. 'Give it mouth!'
'Pip. Pip, sir.'
'Show us where you live,' said the man. 'Point out the place!'
I pointed to where our village lay, on the flat in-shore among the alder-trees and pollards, a mile or more from the church.

The man, after looking at me for a moment, turned me upside down, and emptied my pockets. There was nothing in them but a piece of bread. When the church came to itself – for he was so sudden and strong that he made it go head over heels before me, and I saw the steeple under my feet – when the church came to itself, I say, I was seated on a high tombstone, trembling, while he ate the bread ravenously.

'You young dog,' said the man, licking his lips, 'what fat cheeks you ha' got.'

I believe they were fat, though I was at that time undersized, for my years, and not strong.

'Darn me if I couldn't eat 'em,' said the man, with a threatening shake of his head, 'and if I han't half a mind to't!'

I earnestly expressed my hope that he wouldn't, and held tighter to the tombstone on which he had put me; partly, to keep myself upon it; partly, to keep myself from crying.

'Now lookee here!' said the man. 'Where's your mother?'
'There, sir!' said I.
He started, made a short run, and stopped and looked over his shoulder.
'There, sir!' I timidly explained. 'Also Georgiana. That's my mother.'
'Oh!' said he, coming back. 'And is that your father alonger your mother?'
'Yes, sir,' said I; 'him too; late of this parish.'
'Ha!' he muttered then, considering. 'Who d'ye live with – supposin' you're kindly let to live, which I han't made up my mind about ?'
'My sister, sir – Mrs Joe Gargery – wife of Joe Gargery, the blacksmith, sir.'
'Blacksmith, eh?' said he. And looked down at his leg.
After darkly looking at his leg and at me several times, he came closer to my tombstone, took me by both arms, and tilted me back as far as he

could hold me; so that his eyes looked most powerfully down into mine, and mine looked most helplessly up into his.

'Now lookee here,' he said, 'the question being whether you're to be let to live. You know what a file is?'

'Yes, sir.'

'And you know what wittles is?'

'Yes, sir.'

After each question he tilted me over a little more, so as to give me a greater sense of helplessness and danger.

'You get me a file.' He tilted me again. 'And you get me wittles.' He tilted me again. 'You bring 'em both to me.' He tilted me again. 'Or I'll have your heart and liver out.' He tilted me again.

I was dreadfully frightened, and so giddy that I clung to him with both hands, and said, 'If you would kindly please to let me keep upright, sir, perhaps I shouldn't be sick, and perhaps I could attend more.'

He gave me a most tremendous dip and roll, so that the church jumped over its own weather-cock. Then, he held me by the arms in an upright position on the top of the stone, and went on in these fearful terms:

'You bring me, tomorrow morning early, that file and them wittles. You bring the lot to me, at that old Battery over yonder. You do it, and you never dare to say a word or dare to make a sign concerning your having seen such a person as me, or any person sum-ever, and you shall be let to live. You fail, or you go from my words in any partickler, no matter how small it is, and your heart and your liver shall be tore out, roasted and ate. Now, I ain't alone, as you may think I am. There's a young man hid with me, in comparison with which young man I am a Angel. That young man hears the words I speak. That young man has a secret way percooliar to himself, of getting at a boy, and at his heart and at his liver. A boy may lock his door, may be warm in bed, may tuck himself up, may draw the clothes over his head, may think himself comfortable and safe, but that young man will softly creep and creep his way to him and tear him open.

Questions

Checking the facts

❶ Who and where is Georgiana?

❷ Why does the man turn Pip upside down?

❸ When Pip says 'There, sir!' (line 31, p.40), why does the man start to run off?

❹ 'Wittles' (line 6, this page) is the man's way of pronouncing 'victuals'.
What are 'victuals'?

❺ 'There's a young man hid with me' (line 25, this page).
Who do you think this is?

A *Which are the key moments of drama in the passage?*

WRITE ABOUT

- the sudden arrival of the man
- the man's physical treatment of Pip
- Pip's words that he lives with the blacksmith
- the threats made towards Pip.

 B *What are Pip's feelings during this scene in the graveyard?*

COMMENT UPON

- his state of mind at the start
- his first reaction to the convict
- the conversation about the file and 'wittles'
- how he feels when the convict is telling him about the other 'young man'.

 C *This extract comes in chapter one of the novel. The convict becomes very important in Pip's later life. How does Charles Dickens make the convict come so alive, for both Pip and the reader?*

DISCUSS

- the convict's physical appearance
- his movements
- his language, particularly the dialect
- the way in which the author creates the convict's sense of desperation.

Grammar Spelling Punctuation

Reported speech

Study the fourth paragraph, on pages 40 and 41. Note how Dickens follows strictly the rules governing the setting out of dialogue.

- Now rewrite those lines removing the direct speech. Retell what happens in straight prose narrative ('reported speech'). What is lost (or gained) in your version?

Writing

In the extract above, Dickens describes the deep desperation felt by the hunted convict.

- Write your own short story of no more than 400 words about a chase of some kind. You could tell the story from your point of view or somebody else's.

KIDNAPPED

FROM A NOVEL BY

ROBERT LOUIS STEVENSON

Learning objectives

- to understand how a writer creates tension and suspense
- to understand how a pre-1900 writer uses certain vocabulary and narrative techniques

Discussion

- What stories – from folk tales, fiction or real life – can you recall in which one member of a family tries to cheat another?
- Do you think that the reading of a will often creates family tensions?

THE STORY SO FAR

Seventeen year-old David Balfour's parents have died; he is given a letter (said to contain his inheritance) to deliver to his uncle Ebenezer Balfour of Shaws. Ebenezer is not pleased to see him. He sends him to fetch a chest from the tower – but refuses to give him a light …

Out I went into the night. The wind was still moaning in the distance, though never a breath of it came near the house of Shaws. It had fallen blacker than ever; and I was glad to feel along the wall, till I came the length of the stair-tower door at the far end of the unfinished wing. I had got the key into the keyhole and had just turned it, when all upon a sudden, without sound of wind or thunder, the whole sky lighted up with wild-fire and went black again. I had to put my hand over my eyes to get back to the colour of the darkness; and indeed I was already half blinded when I stepped into the tower.

It was so dark inside, it seemed a body could scarce breathe; but I pushed out with foot and hand, and presently struck the wall with the one, and the lowermost round of the stair with the other. The wall, by the touch, was of fine hewn stone; the steps too, though somewhat steep and narrow, were of polished masonwork, and regular and solid under foot. Minding my uncle's word about the banisters, I kept close to the tower side, and felt my way in the pitch darkness with a beating heart.

The house of Shaws stood some five full storeys high, not counting lofts. Well, as I advanced, it seemed to me the stair grew airier and a thought more lightsome; and I was wondering what might be the cause of this change, when a second blink of the summer lightning came and went. If I did not cry out, it was because fear had me by the throat; and if I did not fall, it was more by Heaven's mercy than my own strength. It was not only that the flash shone in on every side through breaches in the wall, so that I seemed to be clambering aloft upon an open scaffold, but the same passing brightness showed me the steps were of unequal length, and that one of my feet rested that moment within two inches of the well.

This was the grand stair! I thought; and with the thought, a gust of a kind of angry courage came into my heart. My uncle had sent me here, certainly to run great risks, perhaps to die. I swore I would settle that 'perhaps', if I should break my neck for it; got me down upon my hands and knees; and as slowly as a snail, feeling before me every inch, and testing the solidity of every stone, I continued to ascend the stair. The darkness, by contrast with the flash, appeared to have redoubled; nor was that all, for my ears were now troubled and my mind confounded by a great stir of bats in the top part of the tower, and the foul beasts, flying downwards, sometimes beat about my face and body.

The tower, I should have said, was square; and in every corner the step was made of a great stone of a different shape, to join the flights.

Well, I had come close to one of these turns, when, feeling forward as usual, my hand slipped upon an edge and found nothing but emptiness beyond it. The stair had been carried no higher: to set a stranger mounting it in the darkness was to send him straight to his death; and (although thanks to the lightning and my own precautions, I was safe enough) the mere thought of the peril in which I might have stood, and the dreadful height I might have fallen from, brought out the sweat upon my body and relaxed my joints.

But I knew what I wanted now, and turned and groped my way down again, with a wonderful anger in my heart. About half-way down, the wind sprang up in a clap and shook the tower, and died again; the rain followed; and before I had reached the ground level it fell in buckets. I put out my head into the storm, and looked along towards the kitchen. The door, which I had shut behind me when I left, now stood open, and shed a little glimmer of light; and I thought I could see a figure standing in the rain, quite still, like a man hearkening. And then there came a blinding flash, which showed me my uncle plainly, just where I had fancied him to stand; and hard upon the heels of it, a great tow-row of thunder.

Now, whether my uncle thought the crash to be the sound of my fall, or whether he heard it in God's voice denouncing murder, I will leave you to guess. Certain it is, at least, that he was seized on by a kind of panic fear, and that he ran into the house and left the door open behind him. I followed as softly as I could, and, coming unheard into the kitchen, stood and watched him.

He had found time to open the corner cupboard and bring out a great case bottle of aqua vitae, and now sat with his back towards me at the table. Ever and again he would be seized with a fit of deadly shuddering and groan aloud, and carrying the bottle to his lips, drink down the raw spirits by the mouthful.

I stepped forward, came close behind him where he sat, and suddenly clapping my two hands down upon his shoulders – ' Ah!' cried I.

My uncle gave a kind of broken cry like a sheep's bleat, flung up his arms, and tumbled to the floor like a dead man.

Questions

Checking the facts

❶ Describe the weather on this night.

❷ What is meant by 'the stair grew airier and a thought more lightsome' (line 4, p.44)?

❸ What precaution saves David's life?

❹ What causes David to break out in a sweat?

 How does Stevenson describe the night and the storm?

WRITE ABOUT

● the wind and rain

● the lightning

● the darkness

● the bats.

What picture do you have of David Balfour and his state of mind in this passage?

COMMENT UPON

● his climb in the tower
● his inner feelings
● his thoughts about his uncle.

 What narrative techniques does Stevenson use to make his reader want to read on?

DISCUSS

● David's step-by-step ascent and descent of the tower
● the impact of the outside elements upon the action
● the use of the first-person narrator
● the length of phrases, clauses and sentences.

Grammar Spelling Punctuation

Figurative language

Look at the following phrases:

'the wind was still moaning' (line 1, p.43)
'the whole sky lighted up with wild-fire' (line 6, p.43)
'fear had me by the throat' (line 7, p.44)
'angry courage came into my heart' (line 15, p.44)
'the darkness appeared to have redoubled' (line 20, p.44)
'a wonderful anger in my heart' (line 35, p.44)
'God's voice denouncing murder' (line 6, p.45)
'a kind of broken cry like a sheep's bleat' (line 18, p.45)

● Language is used here both *figuratively* and *literally*. Pick three of these expressions and discuss with a partner the picture that each one creates in your mind's eye.

Writing

Use one of the following phrases as the opening sentence in a story of your own. Aim for about 300–400 words.

● Fear had me by the throat.
● Angry courage came into my heart.

THE FLOWERS

A SHORT STORY BY ALICE WALKER

Learning objectives

- to understand how a writer describes a single scene
- to understand how a writer makes us think about a particular issue

Discussion

- Have you ever – alone – suddenly come across something that has taken you by complete surprise? How did you react?

It seemed to Myop as she skipped lightly from hen house to pigpen to smokehouse that the days had never been as beautiful as these. The air held a keenness that made her nose twitch. The harvesting of the corn and cotton, peanuts and squash, made each day a golden surprise that caused excited little tremors to run up her jaws.

Myop carried a short, knobby stick. She struck out at random at chickens she liked, and worked out the beat of a song on the fence around the pigpen. She felt light and good in the warm sun. She was ten, and nothing existed for her but her song, the stick clutched in her dark brown hand, and the tat-de-ta-ta-ta of accompaniment.

Turning her back on the rusty boards of her family's sharecropper cabin, Myop walked along the fence till it ran into the stream made by the spring. Around the spring, where the family got drinking water, silver ferns and wild flowers grew. Along the shallow banks pigs rooted. Myop watched the tiny white bubbles disrupt the thin black scale of soil and the water that silently rose and slid away down the stream.

She had explored the woods behind the house many times. Often, in late autumn, her mother took her to gather nuts among the fallen leaves. Today she made her own path, bouncing this way and that way, vaguely keeping an eye out for snakes. She found, in addition to various common but pretty ferns and leaves, an armful of strange blue flowers with velvety ridges and a sweetsuds bush full of the brown, fragrant buds.

By twelve o'clock, her arms laden with sprigs of her findings, she was a mile or more from home. She had often been as far before, but the strangeness of the land made it not as pleasant as her usual haunts. It seemed gloomy in the little cover in which she found herself. The air was damp, the silence close and deep.

Myop began to circle back to the house, back to the peacefulness of the morning. It was then she stepped smack into his eyes. Her heel became lodged in the broken ridge between brow and nose, and she reached down quickly, unafraid, to free herself. It was only when she saw his naked grin that she gave a little yelp of surprise.

He had been a tall man. From feet to neck covered a long space. His head lay beside him. When she pushed back the leaves and layers of earth and debris Myop saw that he'd had large white teeth, all of them cracked or broken, long fingers, and very big bones. All his clothes had rotted away except some threads of blue denim from his overalls. The buckles of the overalls had turned green.

Myop gazed around the spot with interest. Very near where she'd stepped into the head was a wild pink rose. As she picked it to add to her bundle she noticed a raised mound, a ring, around the rose's root. It was the rotted remains of a noose, a bit of shredding plowline, now blending benignly into the soil. Around an overhanging limb of a great spreading oak clung another piece. Frayed, rotted, bleached, and frazzled – barely there – but spinning restlessly in the breeze. Myop laid down her flowers.

And the summer was over.

Questions

Checking the facts

❶ What time of year is it in the story?
❷ Where does Myop live?
❸ How far from home does she wander?
❹ What does she catch her foot in?
❺ What has happened to the dead man?

A *What are the key events in this story?*

WRITE ABOUT

- Myop setting off from home
- her walk into the woods
- her finding of the body
- her laying down of the flowers.

 B *Why do you think Alice Walker wrote this story?*

COMMENT UPON

- the descriptions in the early paragraphs
- how Myop reacts to what happens (think about her name)
- the way the man has died
- the closing lines of the story.

 C *What story-telling skills make 'The Flowers' a convincing short story?*

DISCUSS

- how the tale begins and ends
- the length of sentences and paragraphs
- the sights and smells Myop meets
- your own thoughts about the story.

Grammar Spelling Punctuation

Nouns and adjectives

Well-chosen describing words (adjectives) are very important to an author as she 'paints her picture'.

- From this story make a list of ten nouns and their linked adjectives.
  For example: 'golden surprise' (line 4, p.47); 'velvety ridges' (line 21, p.47).

- How often in the story does the writer put *two* adjectives with a noun?
  Write down the phrases where she does this.
  For example: 'large white teeth' (line 13, p.48).

- Which three descriptions in the story do you think are especially rich?

Writing

Write your own short story titled 'Discovery'.

- You may want to use a first-person narrator ('I') or a third-person narrator as Alice Walker does in 'The Flowers'.

FIVE HOURS TO SIMLA

FROM A SHORT STORY BY ANITA DESAI

Learning objectives

- to understand how a writer uses events to reveal character
- to understand how a writer uses dialogue in shaping a story

Discussion

- Have you ever been on an especially long journey – on your own, with family, with a group of friends? What memories do you have of its highlights and frustrations?

THE STORY SO FAR

This passage begins a short story by the Indian writer Anita Desai.

Then, miraculously, out of the pelt of yellow fur that was the dust growing across the great northern Indian plain, a wavering grey line emerged. It might have been a cloud bank looming, but it was not – the sun blazed, the earth shrivelled, the heat burnt away every trace of spring's beneficence. Yet the grey darkened, turned bluish, took on substance.

'Look – mountains!'

'Where?'

'I can't see any mountains.'

'Are you blind?' Look, look up – not down, fool!'

A scuffle broke out between the boys on the sticky grime of the Rexine-covered front seat. It was quietened by a tap on their heads from their mother in the back. 'Yes, yes, mountains. The Himalayas. We'll be there soon.'

'Huh.' A sceptical grunt from the driver of the tired, dust-buried grey Ambassador car. 'At least five more hours to Simla.' He ran his hand over the back of his neck where all the dirt of the road seemed to have found its way under the wilting cotton collar.

'Sim-la! Sim-la!' the boys set up a chant, their knees bouncing up and down in unison.

Smack, the driver's left hand landed on the closest pair, bringing out an instant stain of red and sudden, sullen silence.

'Be quiet!' the mother hissed from the back unnecessarily.

The Ambassador gave a sudden lurch, throwing everyone forwards. The baby, whose mouth had been glued to the teat of a bottle like a fly to syrup, came unstuck and wailed with indignation. Even their mother let out a small involuntary cry. Her daughter, who had been asleep on the back seat, her legs across her mother's lap, now stirred.

'Accident!' howled the small boy who had been smacked, triumphantly.

But it was not. His father had stopped just short of the bicycle rickshaw ahead, which had just avoided running into the bullock cart carrying farmers' families to market. A bus, loaded with baggage and spilling over with passengers, had also ground to a halt with a shrieking of brakes. Ahead of it was a truck, wrapped and folded in canvas sheets that blocked all else from sight. The mountains had disappeared and so had the road.

After the first cacophony of screeching brakes and grinding gears, there followed the comparatively static hum of engines, and drivers waited in exasperation for the next lurch forwards. For the moment there was a lull, curious on that highway. Then the waiting very quickly began to fray at the edges. The sun was beating on the metal of the vehicles, and the road lay flattened across the parched plain, with no trees to screen it from the sun. First one car horn began to honk, then a bicycle rickshaw began to clang its bell, then a truck blared its musical horn, and then the lesser ones began to go pom-pom, pom-pom almost in harmony, and suddenly, out of the centre of all that noise, a long, piercing wail emerged.

The two boys, the girl, the baby, all sat up, shocked. More so when they saw what their father was doing. Clenching the wheel with both hands, his head was lowered on to it, and the blare of the horn seemed to issue out of his fury.

The mother exclaimed.

The father raised his head and banged on the wheel, struck it. 'How will we get to Simla before dark?' he howled.

The mother exclaimed again, shocked. 'But we'll be moving again in a minute.'

As if to contradict her, the driver of the truck stalled at the top of the line, swung himself out of the cabin into the road. He'd turned off his engine and stood in the deeply rutted dust, fumbling in his shirt pocket for cigarettes.

Other drivers got out of and down from their vehicles: the bullock-cart driver lowered himself from the creaking cart; the bicycle-rickshaw driver descended: the bus driver got out and stalked, in his sweat-drenched khakis, towards the truck driver standing at the head of the line: and they all demanded, 'What's going on? Breakdown?'

The truck driver watched them approach but was lighting his cigarette and didn't answer. Then he waved an arm – his movements were leisurely, elegant, quite unlike what his driving had been – and said, 'Stone throw. Somebody threw a stone. Hit windshield. Cracked it.'

The father in the Ambassador had also joined them in the road. Hands on his hips, he demanded, 'So?'

'So?' said the truck driver, narrowing his eyes. They were grey in a tanned face, heavily outlined and elongated with khol, and his hair was tied up in a bandanna with a long loose end that dangled upon his shoulder. 'So we won't be moving again till the person who did it is caught, and a *faisla* is made – a settlement.'

Immediately a babble broke out. All the drivers flung out their hands and arms in angry, demanding gestures, their voices rose in questioning, in cajoling, in argument. The truck driver stood looking at them, watching them, his face inscrutable. Now and then he lifted the cigarette to his mouth and drew a deep puff. Then abruptly he swung around, clambered back into the cabin of his truck and started the engine with a roar at which the others fell back, their attitudes slackening in relief, but then he wheeled the truck around and parked it squarely across the highway so no traffic could get past in either direction. The highway at that point had narrowed to a small culvert across a dry stream-bed full of stones. Now he clambered up the bank of the culvert and sat down, his legs wide apart in their loose and not too clean pyjamas, regarding the traffic piling up in both directions as though he was watching sheep filing into a pen.

The knot of drivers in the road began to grow, joined by many of the passengers demanding to know the cause of this impasse.

'Dadd-ee! Dadd-ee!' the small boys yelled, hanging out of the door their father had left open and all but falling out into the dust. 'What's happened, Dadd-ee?'

Questions

Checking the facts
❶ How many people are travelling in the car?
❷ What is the Ambassador?
❸ How many different forms of transport appear on the road?
❹ What is the family's destination?
❺ Why has the truck driver caused the hold-up?

What are the main events in this episode as seen by the children?

WRITE ABOUT

- what happens inside their car
- how their mother and father behave
- events on the road, including the 'accident'
- the other drivers.

 Do the man and his wife react in the same way or differently to what happens?

COMMENT UPON

- their actions
- their speech
- their inner thoughts and feelings
- how you picture them as characters.

 What snapshot of her native India is the author giving in this story?

DISCUSS

- the landscape
- the climate
- the people
- the unfolding of events and the truck driver's demand for a 'faisla' (line 13, p.52).

Grammar Spelling Punctuation

Apostrophes for possession

In pairs, look at these phrases and discuss the rule for using the apostrophe to show possession:

'her mother's lap'   'carry farmers' families'.

- Find other examples in this extract of the apostrophe used to show possession.

- Find the two uses of *its* in this extract. In pairs, discuss the difference between *its* and *it's*.

Writing

Write your own 300-word ending to this story.

- Think through how the 'impasse' (line 29, p.52) might be resolved. You could make the next moments take on either a comic or perhaps sinister twist.

THE THWARTING OF BARON BOLLIGREW

FROM A STAGE PLAY BY ROBERT BOLT

Learning objectives

- to understand how a character's main features are important to the story

- to understand how a dramatist sometimes mixes different genres

Discussion

- What do you know about the stories of King Arthur and the Knights of the Round Table? What principles did they fight for? Have you seen any comic films based upon the Middle Ages and knights in armour (such as *Monty Python and the Holy Grail* or the first *Blackadder* series)? What do you find funny in those stories?

THE STORY SO FAR

Sir Oblong Fitz Oblong has been sent over to the Bolligrew Islands to put right the wrongs being done by Baron Bolligrew and his dim henchman, Squire Blackheart. In this scene, Blackheart has come on orders from the Baron to challenge Oblong to a duel …

Oblong: Good evening, Squire.
Blackheart: Tchah!
He advances deliberately, peasants shrinking back, and hurls down his gauntlet.
Oblong: You've dropped your glove.
Blackheart: I've thrown down me gauntlet. Any gentleman'd know that.
Oblong: You want me to fight a duel with you, Squire?
Blackheart: Right.
Oblong: Well, I'm not going to.
Blackheart: Then – *(an effort of memory)* – I'm goin' to insult you!
Oblong: Well please be quick; I have a lot to do and the light's going.
Blackheart: *(studies a grubby scrap of paper)* Oblong, you're a–a, mm … *(He has difficulty in reading.)*
Oblong peers at the paper.

Oblong:	Varlet.
Blackheart:	Right! A varlet! And a, mm...
Oblong:	Knave.
Blackheart:	That's it! Knave and varlet! You – you're not a gentleman! Thought of that meself.
Oblong:	The subject seems to obsess you, Squire.
Blackheart:	*(amazed)* Well, if you won't fight *now* –
Oblong:	No.
Blackheart:	*(nonplussed, consults paper, brow clears)* Well then, your sweaty friends can see what kind of Champion they've *got*! *(To 5th peasant.)* You.
5th Peasant:	*(approaching, humbly)* Yes, Squire?
Blackheart:	Pick up me glove.
5th Peasant:	Yes, Squire. *(Does so.)*

Behind Oblong, peasants lay down sections of church.

Blackheart:	*(going, to Oblong)* And a very good evening to *you*, Fatty!

Exit Blackheart.

Oblong:	*(watching him off)* What a deplorable exhibition! Well now – *(Turns to find peasants going.)* What's the matter? Stop!

Exit peasants, 5th Peasant passing.

	My good friend –
5th Peasant:	Sorry, sir. But if you'm afeared to tackle Squire, we'm afeared to 'elp you. And that's the top and bottom of it, sir.

Exit 5th Peasant.

Oblong:	*(to Lord Mayor)* I'm not afraid of the Squire!
Lord Mayor:	No, No. Of course not.
Oblong:	But duelling is utterly against my principles.
Lord Mayor:	I agree with you, Sir Oblong. I agree with you. *(But he is backing towards the Exit.)*
Oblong:	Well, the two of us must just do what we can, eh? *(attempts to lift large segment of church)* Would you –?
Lord Mayor:	The fact is, sir, I ought to be getting back to the shop. I'm sorry, Sir Oblong, really I am …

Exit Lord Mayor.

Oblong:	Dash it! *(defiantly)* Yes – I am not often intemperate in my language but dash it! … What shall I do now? Perhaps I ought to have fought that fellow Blackheart after all? What do you think?

Continues ad lib till audience response strong.

	Might do him good to learn a lesson, eh? In my younger days I was national Broadsword Champion you know, and

Growing excited.

     – and Area Champion three years running!

     After all, he challenged me, didn't he? Perhaps I ought to find the fellow now? Do a little challenging myself? Ha! *(draws sword)* I have at thee for a foul caitiff! Take that – and that – anthatanthatanthat!

When response maximum, pulls himself up.

     No. No. *(sheathes sword)* Certainly not. I have been sent here to set a good example. You ought to be ashamed of yourselves. Duelling, is *wrong* … I must manage somehow by myself. *(attempts to lift segment of church)* No … Now let's see … No … You know at this point in the story I do think they might send *somebody* to help me.

Enter unseen by him Magpie.

     However … Keep trying … No.

Voice from audience: Behind you!

Oblong: What? Try a smaller piece? Right. Now, then … No … I really don't see how I'm going to manage, you know … How about this bit …?

And so on, till audience response strong. Then turns, sees Magpie.

Oblong: Oh. Good evening.

Magpie: My name's Mike Magpie. Your name's Oblong. You saved my life this morning an' you can count on me. Anythin' in the thieving line now, or the telling lies line, or the leading up the garden path line –

Oblong: Did you say 'thieving'? Stealing is *wrong*.

Questions

Checking the facts

❶ Why does Blackheart throw down his gauntlet?

❷ What is written on Blackheart's piece of paper? Why does he keep checking it?

❸ Why does Oblong refuse to fight him?

❹ Why do the peasants and the Lord Mayor refuse to help rebuild the church?

❺ Why is Magpie keen to help Oblong?

A *Recount the very different experiences that Oblong has in this short extract.*

WRITE ABOUT

- Squire Blackheart's challenge
- the reaction of the peasants and Lord Mayor
- his meeting with Magpie.

 B *Oblong is famous for his strict principles. What are they and what importance do they have for the story?*

COMMENT UPON

- his refusal to take up Blackheart's challenge and the effect this has on other characters
- his discussion with the audience about fighting
- his attitude to Magpie's thieving.

 C *How has Robert Bolt combined the elements of a medieval 'knights-in-armour' story with the style of a pantomime?*

DISCUSS

- the features of the play (characters and incidents) which are typical of stories about knights in armour
- the characters more usually found in pantomime
- the features of the style of performance which are typical of pantomime.

Grammar Spelling Punctuation

Concrete nouns and proper nouns

Write a c or p next to the following ten nouns, to show whether they are concrete nouns or proper nouns:

Squire	Oblong	glove	gauntlet	gentleman
Blackheart	varlet	knave	friends	Fatty

- Pick out further concrete and proper nouns from the extract. Which ones are especially important in *labelling* characters?

Writing

Write the letter that Oblong sends back to the court, updating them on his mission.

- You could express opinions on Squire Blackheart's behaviour; explain why you did not accept his challenge; write about the difficulties facing you; and describe your meeting with Magpie.

57

FRANKENSTEIN

FROM A STAGE PLAY ADAPTED BY PHILIP PULLMAN
FROM A NOVEL BY MARY SHELLEY

Learning objectives

- to understand how a character's feelings are conveyed in a play
- to understand how a playwright creates sympathy for a character

Discussion

- Have you seen any of the film versions of *Frankenstein?* What image did it create of the monster? Is it right to try to create life in the way Frankenstein does?

THE STORY SO FAR

Having created a human-like monster, Dr Frankenstein is shocked by what he has done. The monster escapes and then news comes that Frankenstein's little brother has been found murdered. The monster returns to confront his creator …

Frankenstein: Monster! I didn't create you to do evil – why have you betrayed me?

Monster: I – betray you? If I knew how to laugh, Frankenstein, I'd shake the house with scorn. *You* are the betrayer – you created me, and you made sure I could never be happy. Isn't that betrayal?

Frankenstein: No! I swear it wasn't like that. I made you, yes –

Monster: And as soon as you saw what you'd done, you turned away in horror and left me to find my own way through the world – a creature everyone turned from with disgust and loathing – a vision from a nightmare! But do you know the cruellest thing of all? It was that I wanted to love. I came to life full of goodwill and friendship for every living creature – I wanted to help them and protect them and give them all the love I felt for them – and when I tried, they stoned me and shot at me and set their dogs on me – and even the dogs turned away in disgust ... Frankenstein, has any man in history ever been more cruel than you have been to me?

Frankenstein: You killed my little brother! Is that love? Is that good will?
Monster: Listen! And I'll tell you everything.

He releases Frankenstein, who falls into the chair. The Monster walks up and down as he speaks; Frankenstein hides his head in his hands, occasionally looking up to reply – the very picture of despair.

Monster: When I came to life I knew nothing. I didn't know who I was, I didn't know what the world was – things had no names. The only thing I knew was pain, but I didn't know what that was till much later, when I found out what it was called. Everything was new, Frankenstein. Do you know how beautiful things are when they're new? Or have you forgotten?

Frankenstein: Get on …

Monster: Ah, yes. I went down into the town, and they called out their dogs. Creatures full of beauty, with soft fur and bright eyes – I wanted to kneel down and pet them and play with them, but they tore at me with their teeth, and then I knew fear for the first time. I ran to the forest, where it was quiet, where there was cool water to bathe my flesh. The moon came up – oh, Frankenstein, to see the moon for the first time! And I found out what sadness was, and loneliness. Those other beings like myself – they stood upright, like me – they'd thrown stones and shouted harsh words at me, but they had companions, fellows, friends. Couldn't I find a friend? So I began to look …

Frankenstein: Where? Where did you look?

Monster: I found a cottage in the forest where a girl and her brother were living – a blind girl, the only piece of luck I ever had. She couldn't see me. We spoke together; oh, I would have been her slave, I would have helped them and worked for them, I would have done anything if they'd only accepted me – but her brother shot me with his musket as if I were a wild beast. It broke my arm. The bullet's still in my shoulder. That was when I found out what pain was really like. All alone in the icy mountains, weeping, crying with rage and loneliness – Frankenstein, you can't imagine how I suffered. if you could imagine it, you'd be on your knees praying to your God for forgiveness.

Frankenstein: *My* God?

Monster: Your God has nothing to do with me. You are my God. You made me, and you owe me happiness. Listen, and I'll tell you the last part of my story. When my wound healed, the bitterness and hatred ebbed away a little; I was still ready to love, still ready to trust ... you see what you'd made, Frankenstein? A creature better than yourself, perhaps? A nature more noble? Who knows what might have happened if ... well, I was more cunning by then. More cautious. I thought – it's only grown men and women who hate me; they've learned to be suspicious and to think the worst of people. But if I could find a child, a little innocent creature with no hatred in its heart, then I could take it with me to the wilderness and bring it up as my companion – and we should love each other and live in peace and goodwill with all living creatures –

Frankenstein: No! No – not my brother –

Monster: I found such a child – a creature like an angel, playing on his own beside the lake. I took his arm – oh, gently, Frankenstein, I had no wish to hurt him. I said, 'Come with me, little one' – and he looked at me, and he screamed – I said, 'No, hush, I shan't hurt you, but you must come with me' – and he said 'I shall tell my brother, Herr Frankenstein! He'll punish you, ugly monster!'

Frankenstein: Oh, no – no –

Monster: I put my hands to his mouth to silence him, because I was afraid. And your name resounded through my head. You, the creator of my misery. You, the source of all my unhappiness. Frankenstein, a name to curse forever! And in that moment I thought – Frankenstein is my enemy, and I can hurt him. I can destroy what is his. I can make you as unhappy as he has made me – and I killed your brother, and I laughed! Yes! The one time I have ever laughed.

Questions

Checking the facts

❶ What was Frankenstein's reaction as soon as he had created the monster?

❷ What was the reaction of the local townsfolk to their first sight of the monster?

❸ What feelings did the monster have when he first approached other people?

❹ Why did he want to find a child, rather than an adult?

❺ How did the monster learn that the child was Frankenstein's brother?

A *What happened after the monster first came to life?*

WRITE ABOUT

- his first visit to the town
- what he did in the days that followed
- what happened when he met Frankenstein's little brother.

 B *What feelings did the monster experience after he was brought to life?*

COMMENT UPON

- his attitudes towards the new things he sees around him
- his experience of pain
- his need for companionship.

 C *In what ways does the story encourage the audience to feel sympathy for the monster?*

DISCUSS

- the language the monster uses to describe people's reactions to him
- the way he talks about his responses to new experiences, such as his first sight of dogs or the moon
- the monster's loneliness
- his motives when he approached the child.

Grammar Spelling Punctuation

Abstract nouns

Abstract nouns are the labels we give to things you cannot touch, such as feelings, ideas or emotions.

- Pick out the abstract nouns in the speech beginning '*And as soon as you saw …*'. Find three which label the bad feelings people had about the monster and three which label the good qualities he wanted to show.

- Look through the rest of the extract and note the importance of the abstract nouns in letting us know what the monster experienced. Make two lists, one of positive qualities such as happiness, the other of negative qualities such as sadness.

Writing

Write a letter from one of the townsfolk to a friend, describing your first sight of the monster, how you felt and what happened.

- You could be one of the townsfolk who attacked the monster, or one who felt sympathy for him. Decide what your reactions could be to his appearance and behaviour.

61

RED DWARF: PSIRENS

FROM A TELEVISION SCRIPT BY
ROB GRANT AND DOUG NAYLOR

Learning objectives

- to understand how science fiction script-writers can create their own, believable world

- to understand how writers use different kinds of comedy

Discussion

- What is science fiction? Discuss examples of as many different kinds of science fiction stories as you can think of. How many science fiction films do you know which contain humour?

THE STORY SO FAR

The crew of Red Dwarf, a gigantic deep-space mining ship, have been in Deep Sleep for two hundred years. At the beginning of the episode, Lister is waking up while Kryten the android is tidying the ship …

1. Observation deck

Dark. Various consoles click into life as we pan round the room, and come to rest on two deep sleep units. Suddenly one of them flares with blue light from inside, and its hood hisses back, revealing a slowly-waking bearded Lister, wearing soiled long johns. He sits up. His mouth tastes vile. He notices his fingernails and toenails are six inches long. Lister pads across the room, and starts to cut his nails in a desk-mounted pencil sharpener. He catches his reflection in a blank TV screen.

Lister: *(to his reflection)* Who the hell are you?

2. Starbug engine room

Kryten empties some waste into a large hatch marked: 'Waste Compactor' and presses the start button. Crushing sounds. He opens the hatch and takes out the garbage, now in a perfect cube.

3. Mid-section of Starbug

More hi-tech than before. Light panels line the back wall. Switches, radar screens, etc. There is a large flatbed scanner screen, which doubles as a table, surrounded by four chairs. Kryten climbs up the spiral staircase with the waste cube. Lister is standing there, looking a bit nonplussed.

Kryten:	Welcome back on-line, sir. How are you feeling?
Lister:	I can't remember anything. I don't know who I am. What is this place? Who are you?

As he speaks, Kryten places the cube in a waste disposal chute and launches it into space.

Kryten:	Ah, you have a touch of amnesia. That's quite common after such a long period in Deep Sleep. You've been out for just over two hundred years.
Lister:	Two hundred years?
Kryten:	Actually, I woke you last spring, but you absolutely insisted on another three months.
Lister:	What did you say my name was?
Kryten:	Lister, sir.
Lister:	And you are – ?
Kryten:	Kryten. I was just preparing your breakfast tray.

Lister examines the tray.

Lister:	These cornflakes have got grated raw onions sprinkled over them.
Kryten:	That's how you like them, sir.
Lister:	Do I? *(sips from glass; winces)* This orange juice is revolting.
Kryten:	That's not orange juice, sir. That's your early-morning pick-me-up. Chilled vindaloo sauce.
Lister:	I drink cold curry sauce for breakfast?
Kryten:	Depends on your mood. If you get up in the afternoon, you often prefer to start the day with a can of last night's flat lager. That's why you sleep with a tea strainer by your bed: to sieve out the cigar dimps.
Lister:	I drink, I smoke, I have curry sauce for breakfast? Raw onions on my cereal? I sound like some barely human grossed-out slime ball.
Kryten:	Oh excellent, sir. It's all flooding back then?
Lister:	No. None of it is.

Kryten hands Lister his guitar.

Lister:	Is this mine? Do I play the guitar?
Kryten:	Do you play the guitar? Do I have a head shaped like an amusing ice cube? Why don't you chock out a few power chords? See if anything comes back to you.

Lister plucks tunelessly at the strings.

Kryten: The Axeman's back!

Lister: Don't patronize me. I can't play the guitar. Anyone with half an ear can tell that.

Kryten: Please, sir – you are not yourself at present. When you're fully functional, and your personality's restored, you will firmly believe you can play the guitar like the ghost of Hendrix.

Questions

Checking the facts

❶ Where is the story set?

❷ Why does Lister have a beard and long fingernails at the beginning of the episode?

❸ Why doesn't he know who he is?

❹ What does Lister usually have for breakfast?

❺ What do we know about Lister's ability to play the guitar?

A What do we know about Lister?

WRITE ABOUT

- what he looks like when he comes out of Deep Sleep
- what he usually eats and drinks
- what he feels about his own guitar playing.

B What kind of world do the crew of Red Dwarf inhabit?

COMMENT UPON

- the waste-disposal system
- the Deep-Sleep technology
- Kryten and the jobs he performs
- how likely it is that such technology could ever exist.

C What different kinds of humour are there in this extract?

DISCUSS

- visual humour: things that make us laugh because of the way they look (such as some of Lister's behaviour)
- verbal humour, which depends upon unexpected things that characters say
- witty or pointed comments from characters (for example, Kryten)
- humour that comes from the situations or the characters' actions
- comedy which results from the mixture of visual and sound effects (as with Lister's guitar).

Grammar Spelling Punctuation

Revising adjectives

An adjective should be used carefully to enable us to understand more about the noun.

- In pairs, find the adjectives which accompany the nouns in the following phrases from the extract and discuss in each case how effective they are:

'with .... light from inside.'   'grated .... onion sprinkled over them.'

'a slowly-waking, ... Lister'   'I drink .... curry sauce for breakfast?'

'in a ....-.......... pencil sharpener.'   'shaped like an .... ice cube?'

'now in a .... cube.'

Writing

Write up the ship's log for that day, as it might be written by Kryten.

- You could write about the incidents portrayed in the extract, or make up others of your own. Use your own style of writing or try to imitate the way Kryten speaks.

65

SILAS MARNER

FROM A STAGE PLAY ADAPTED BY JOHN O'CONNOR
FROM A NOVEL BY GEORGE ELIOT

Learning objectives

- to understand how we learn about character through the dialogue

- to understand how a play can give an impression of a whole society

Discussion

- Have you ever been accused of something of which you were innocent? Do you know of incidents where that has happened to other people? Which historical characters have suffered in this way?

THE STORY SO FAR

Silas Marner has had to leave his home village, having been falsely accused of stealing some money from a dying old man. In this scene Silas experiences one of his 'visitations', a sort of trance, in which he dreams about the incident …

Scene 6

Marner's cottage. We hear the violin note which tells us that he is experiencing a seizure.

[1] *A church official*

Silas: William always came to relieve me at two … I would sit with the old archdeacon[1] while he slept and then William would come. But that night, the night the old man died, William failed to arrive … And when I woke, the archdeacon was dead and … *(as though finding it difficult to understand, even after all these years)* And they wanted to see me in the assembly house … They were all gathered there when I arrived … The minister, William, the church elders and … and Sarah, my Sarah was there too … I remember how she looked at me … How she looked when the minister spoke …

The minister's voice is heard as Silas hears it in his head, echoing loudly.

Minister: Silas, is this your pocket knife?

Although deep in a trance, Silas speaks his responses aloud.

Silas:	Yes. Where –?
Minister:	Silas, you cannot hide your sin. Confess and repent.
Silas:	My sin?
Minister:	The knife was found in the chest by the departed archdeacon's bedside, Silas. The chest wherein had lain the church savings. I saw that bag of money myself only yesterday. But this morning the bag is gone. Some hand removed that money.
Silas:	No!
Minister:	And whose hand could it be, if not that of the man to whom the knife belonged?
Silas:	God will clear me. I know nothing of the knife being there, or the money being gone. Search me and my dwelling. You will find nothing but three pound five of my own savings, which William Dane knows I have had these six months.
Minister:	The proof is heavy against you, brother Marner. William Dane declares that he was hindered by sickness from going to relieve you as usual. And you yourself said that he had not come. And moreover you neglected the dead body.
Silas:	I must have slept … *(after a pause)* Or I must have had another visitation like that which you all saw me under once in chapel, so that the thief must have come and gone while I was not in the body, but out of the body. But I say again, search me and my dwelling, for I have been nowhere else.
Minister:	Brother Marner. William Dane has searched your dwellings. The money was found there.
Dane:	*(showing Silas the bag of money)* Confess, brother. You know it is wrong to hide your sins.
Silas:	William. For nine long years that we have gone in and out together, have you ever known me tell a lie? But God will clear me.
Dane:	Brother, how do I know what you may have done in the secret chambers of your heart, when Satan had an advantage over you?
Sarah:	I can forgive you, Silas, if you repent. But you must know that our engagement is at an end.
Silas:	Sarah –
Minister:	Brother Marner. As is the custom, we have prayed for guidance and have submitted ourselves to the drawing of lots[2], in the knowledge that the Lord will show his truth through the lots drawn. Will you accept that judgement, Silas?
Silas:	I will accept it. The powers above will show me to be innocent.

2 *Letting chance decide whether he is guilty.*

67

The minister has a bag, out of which each of the brethren in turn takes a pebble, some white, some black. They process towards William Dane and drop their pebbles, one by one into an earthenware pot, which he holds out towards them. After the last lot has been cast, Dane empties the pot on the ground. Dane separates the pebbles and we see that nearly all of them are black. The congregation begin their echoing whisper of 'Guilty!', which will grow louder over the next speeches.

Dane:	The lots declare you to be guilty, Silas.
Silas:	*(suddenly realising the truth)* William! The last time I recall using my knife was when I took it out to cut a strap for you. I don't remember putting it in my pocket again.
Dane:	What are you saying, Silas?
Silas:	You stole the money! You stole it and you have woven a plot to lay the sin at my door. But you may prosper for all that. The lots have spoken falsely. There is no just God that governs the earth righteously, but a God of lies, that bears witness against the innocent!

3 A sin against religion

There is a general shout of anger as the voices cry 'Blasphemy! Blasphemy!' [3], then fade to silence.

Dane:	I leave our brethren to judge whether this is the voice of Satan or not. I can do nothing but pray for you, Silas.
Minister:	Brother Marner. You are suspended from chapel-membership, and I call upon you to render up the stolen money. Only on confession, as a sign of repentance, will you be accepted back into the fold.
Silas:	*(Looks at both of them and then around at the imagined assembly of church elders.)* I cannot remain here with despair in my soul.
Sarah:	May the Lord guide you to a clearer way, Silas.
Silas:	*(bitterly)* A clearer way. Yes. A clearer way.

Questions

Checking the facts

❶ Which object was first produced as evidence?

❷ Why did it seem to be proof that Silas had stolen the money?

❸ Why couldn't Silas recall whether William Dane had come to relieve him as usual?

❹ What final evidence is produced by William Dane to seal Silas's fate?

❺ What does Dane say about Silas's trances which might account for Silas's 'crime'?

A *What actually seems to have happened the night Silas was watching over the dying man and the following morning?*

WRITE ABOUT

- the usual arrangement between Silas and William Dane

- Silas's strange seizures

- what William Dane seems to have done during the night and the next morning to make it appear as though Silas stole the money.

 B *What do we learn about Silas from this extract?*

COMMENT UPON

- Silas's innocent bewilderment

- his faith in God and the procedures in chapel

- his seizures

- his realisation towards the end of what has actually happened.

 C *What picture does the play give of the society in which this incident takes place?*

DISCUSS

- what we learn – from the language the characters use and the things they do – about the period in which the story is set

- what we learn about the community's religious practices

- what we learn about people's religious beliefs and attitudes.

Grammar Spelling Punctuation

Revising verbs

Verbs are usually the most important part of a sentence.

- Look at the verbs in Silas's first speech and then, in pairs, take it in turns to speak the speech, with actions, *using only the verbs*:
  'came to relieve … would sit … slept … would come.
  died … failed to arrive … woke … was dead …
  wanted to see … were gathered … arrived …
  was … remember … looked … spoke.'

Writing

Write a newspaper article headlined 'Local weaver convicted of theft'.

- You could write in the style of the extract, using the kind of language the characters use; try to include some quotes from the Minister, Sarah or William Dane.

THE COMPUTER NUT

FROM A RADIO PLAY ADAPTED BY MARCY KAHAN
FROM A NOVEL BY BETSY BYARS

Learning objectives

- to understand how characters' different attitudes can be conveyed through dialogue

- to understand how a play written for radio differs from one written for the stage

Discussion

- How many films have you seen in which aliens secretly visit Earth? What are the reasons usually given to explain the aliens' unwillingness to be seen by everybody? In the films, what kinds of people usually make friends with the aliens and help them?

THE STORY SO FAR

BB9, an alien, is visiting Earth as he has heard that it is the only planet where people laugh. Unfortunately, as he explains to Kate and Willie, the two teenagers he has contacted through their computers, his own first attempts at humour have not been successful, especially when he decides he should make his jokes more personal …

Scene 8: Outside Burger's

Kate: Willie, this is BB9, and he is for real.

BB9:   Glad to meet you, Willie. My, you are fat. I bet you get fan mail from elephants. *(shouting to passersby)* Hey, Lady, you are so bowlegged you could walk down a bowling alley *during* the game!

Kate: Come on, Willie. We'd better get him out of here.

BB9:   Why? I am not funny? What is happening with these unsmiling people?

Scene 9: Suburban street

BB9:   This is not at all as I imagined. I am now ninety minutes into my visit, Earth time, and not one single laugh, no pies on the face, no slips on banana peels. What is it with this planet?

Kate: Look, BB9 – there's my house. The lights are on in the basement. That means my dad's playing with his model trains. You promised to meet him, remember? This is really important to me. Please!

Willie: Dr Morrison's a very nice man, BB9. I can't honestly say he's a barrel of laughs, but he –

BB9: Dr Morrison? Your father is a doctor?

Kate: Yes.

BB9: Then I will come in for a moment. Medical jokes are one of my specialities.

Kate: Come on. It's this way.

FX[1] *Door opening and shutting.*

Kate: Dad?

Dr Morrison: *(from basement)* Just a minute, Kate.

Scene 10: Morrison's basement

(FX, Dr Morrison, Kate, BB9 and Willie)

FX *Trains speeding around track.*

Dr Morrison: Hello, Kate. Willie. You're just in time to help me with the new signals. Now you two stand over there –

Kate: Dad – this is BB9. You saw BB9's picture on the computer. Remember you thought he wasn't real?

Dr Morrison: Oh yes. Well, I'm glad to see that you are. Kate has a lot of fun out of communications. For a while we thought you were going to turn out to be a little green man.

BB9: I assume the colour green only when I visit the planet Chlorophylia. I understand that you are a doctor.

Dr Morrison: Oh no! No you don't. I absolutely refuse to be taken in by this. You are still pretending that this boy is from outer space, right?

Willie: Listen, Dr Morrison, this is for real. I didn't believe it myself at first but –

Dr Morrison: Now I have to admit, Kate, that you have played this whole thing very carefully, very skilfully. You have led up to this moment perfectly. The voice is a master touch, and if your mother were here, she'd fall for it completely.

Kate: Dad!

Willie: Dr Morrison, listen to Kate. She's telling the BB9 truth!

Dr Morrison: This is a super practical joke. *(to BB9)* And it was your idea, young man, wasn't it? Well, I have to congratulate you.

BB9: What do you mean, a super practical joke? What is he

saying, Computer Nut? I have not told the first joke yet. Dr Morrison, how many Plotovian doctors does it take to remove an –

Dr Morrison: Wait, I've got an idea. I'll call your mom. She's over at Boo's playing bridge, and it will only take her two minutes maximum to get home. I think she'll fall for this hook, line and sinker.

BB9: Wait. I thought of a better one. Why do nurses on Plotovia wear pointed hats?

Dr Morrison: *(halfway up the stairs)* Yes sir, she'll get a real kick out of this. See, Kate's mom has been worrying about Kate communicating with you, and she really believes in UFOs. She thought she saw one last summer. I had to stop her from calling the radio station. Now, I won't be a minute.

FX *Sound of footsteps.*

BB9: But sir, I have time for only one or two more tries. Why do the ambulances on Exxyor have square wheels? I am getting worse. This time I did not even get to give a single punch line.

Questions

Checking the facts

❶ In what way is Earth not at all like BB9 imagined?

❷ What is Dr Morrison's first reaction to BB9?

❸ What is Dr Morrison doing when BB9 meets him?

❹ What does Dr Morrison mean when he says that Kate's mother will 'fall for this hook, line and sinker'?

 What does the extract tell us about BB9?

WRITE ABOUT

● his 'personal' jokes

● his reactions when people don't laugh

● his fondness for medical jokes

● the sound of his voice.

What are the main differences between Kate and Willie, on the one hand, and Kate's father on the other, in terms of their attitude towards BB9?

COMMENT UPON

- Kate's belief in BB9

- her reaction to his use of personal jokes

- her father's reaction to meeting BB9

- his references to his wife.

 In what ways has this adaptation been written to make it work as a radio play, rather than a stage play?

DISCUSS

- the use of sound effects

- the movements from one scene location to the next

- the imagined characters who do not have any dialogue

- the movement of characters in and out of locations (e.g. Dr Morrison 'halfway up the stairs').

Grammar Spelling Punctuation

Simple sentences

Because BB9 is speaking a foreign language, he doesn't use many long, complicated sentences.

- In fact, many of his sentences are *simple sentences*: in other words, they contain only one subject and one main verb. For example: 'Your father [s] is [v] a doctor?'

- Pick out the subject and verb in the following simple sentences, taken from the extract:

'My, you are fat.'   'You saw BB9's picture on the computer.'

'I am not funny?'   'You have led up to this moment perfectly.'

'Then I will come in for a moment.'   'This is a super practical joke.'

'Medical jokes are one of my specialities.'

Writing

This extract comes very near the end of the play: there are only two scenes to go. Decide how you think the play should end and write the final scene or two.

- For example, BB9 might stay on Earth to become a more successful comedian, or leave for his own planet. Kate and Willie might persuade people that BB9 is a genuine alien, or decide to keep the whole thing secret.

ANDROCLES AND THE LION

FROM A STAGE PLAY BY BERNARD SHAW

Learning objectives

- to understand how a character's background can be established through the dialogue

- to understand how dialogue and actions can be interpreted in different ways

Discussion

- The story of Androcles and the lion was originally one of Aesop's fables, written in the sixth century BC by a Greek slave. What happens in the original fable?

- What does Jesus have to say about 'turning the other cheek'?

THE STORY SO FAR

The scene is set in a street in ancient Rome, where a group of early Christians are being escorted by some Roman soldiers to the Coliseum, a great stadium, where they will be thrown to the lions or forced to fight gladiators. They are met by a young Roman called Lentulus, who decides to mock one of the Christians, a fearsome ex-warrior called Ferrovius …

Lentulus:	*(indicating the kneeling Ferrovius)* Is this one of the turn-the-other-cheek gentlemen, Centurion?
Centurion:	Yes, sir. Lucky for you too, sir, if you want to take any liberties with him.
Lentulus:	*(to Ferrovius)* You turn the other cheek when youre struck, I'm told.
Ferrovius:	*(slowly turning his great eyes on him)* Yes, by the grace of God, I do, now.
Lentulus:	Not that you're a coward, of course; but of pure piety.[1]
Ferrovius:	I fear God more than man; at least I try to.
Lentulus:	Let's see.

[1] *religious goodness*

He strikes Ferrovius on the cheek. Androcles makes a wild movement to rise and interfere; but Lavinia holds him down, watching Ferrovius intently. Ferrovius, without flinching, turns the other cheek. Lentulus titters foolishly, and strikes him again feebly.

> You know, I should feel ashamed if I let myself be struck like that, and took it lying down. But then I'm not a Christian: I'm a man.

Ferrovius rises impressively and towers over him. Lentulus becomes white with terror; and a shade of green flickers in his cheek for a moment.

Ferrovius: *(with the calm of a steam hammer)* I have not always been faithful. The first man who struck me as you have just struck me was a stronger man than you: he hit me harder than I expected. I was tempted and fell[2]; and it was then that I first tasted bitter shame. I never had a happy moment after that until I had knelt and asked his forgiveness by his bedside in the hospital. *(putting his hands on Lentulus's shoulders)* But now I have learnt to resist with a strength that is not my own. I am not ashamed now, nor angry.

Lentulus: *(uneasily)* Er – good evening. *(He tries to move away.)*

Ferrovius: *(gripping his shoulders)* Oh, do not harden your heart, young man. Come: try for yourself whether our way is not better than yours. I will now strike you on one cheek; and you will turn the other and learn how much better you will feel than if you gave way to the promptings of anger.

Ferrovius holds Lentulus with one hand and clenches the other fist.

Lentulus: Centurion: I call on you to protect me.

Centurion: You asked for it sir. It's no business of ours. Youve had two whacks at him. Better pay him.

Lentulus: Yes, of course. *(to Ferrovius)* It was only a bit of fun, I assure you: I meant no harm. Here. *(He proffers a gold coin.)*

Ferrovius: *(taking it and throwing it to the old beggar, who snatches it up eagerly, and hobbles off to spend it)* Give all thou has to the poor. Come, friend: courage! I may hurt your body for a moment; but your soul will rejoice in the victory of the spirit over the flesh. *(He prepares to strike.)*

Androcles: Easy, Ferrovius, easy: you broke the last man's jaw.

Lentulus, with a moan of terror, attempts to fly; but Ferrovius holds him ruthlessly.

Ferrovius: Yes: but I saved his soul. What matters a broken jaw?

Lentulus: Don't touch me, do you hear? The law –

Ferrovius: The law will throw me to the lions tomorrow: what worse could it do were I to slay you? Pray for strength; and it shall be given to you.

Lentulus: Let me go. Your religion forbids you to strike me.

2 *I gave in to temptation*

Ferrovius:	On the contrary, it commands me to strike you. How can you turn the other cheek, if you are not first struck on the one cheek?
Lentulus:	*(almost in tears)* But I'm convinced already that what you said is quite right. I apologise for striking you.
Ferrovius:	*(greatly pleased)* My son: Have I softened your heart? Has the good seed fallen in a fruitful place? Are your feet turning towards a better path?
Lentulus:	*(abjectly)*[3] Yes, yes. Theres a great deal in what you say.
Ferrovius:	*(radiant)* Join us. Come to the lions. Come to suffering and death.
Lentulus:	*(falling on his knees and bursting into tears)* Oh, help me. Mother! Mother!
Ferrovius:	These tears will water your soul and make it bring forth good fruit, my son. God has greatly blessed my efforts at conversion. Shall I tell you a miracle – yes, a miracle – wrought by me in Cappadocia? A young man – just such a one as you, with golden hair like yours – scoffed at and struck me as you scoffed at and struck me. I sat up all night with that youth wrestling for his soul; and in the morning not only was he a Christian, but his hair was as white as snow. *(Lentulus falls in a dead faint.)* There, there; take him away. The spirit has overwrought him, poor lad. Carry him gently to his house; and leave the rest to heaven.

[3] *very miserably*

Questions

Checking the facts

❶ What does Lentulus mean by: 'You turn the other cheek when you're struck, I'm told.'?

❷ What does Ferrovius do when Lentulus strikes him?

❸ What happened to the first man who struck Ferrovius in this way?

❹ Why doesn't the centurion stop Ferrovius?

❺ What is it that finally makes Lentulus faint?

A *What part does Lentulus play in this episode?*

WRITE ABOUT

- What he does to Ferrovius at the beginning
- why he does it
- what his feelings are towards the end.

 B *What do we learn about Ferrovius in this extract?*

COMMENT UPON

- what he was like before he became a Christian
- what he feels about himself now that he is a Christian
- the way he manages to deal with Lentulus without actually resorting to violence.

 C *How exactly does Ferrovius make Lentulus regret striking him?*

DISCUSS

- the language he uses in describing his previous 'conversions'
- his actions, as described in the stage directions
- whether you feel that he is intentionally exacting revenge upon Lentulus or behaving quite innocently.

Grammar Spelling Punctuation

Apostrophes for abbreviation

Bernard Shaw felt that the apostrophe was usually unnecessary in abbreviations and often left it out.

- Write out the following words from the extract as they would normally appear in standard English: *youre, lets, youve, theres*.

- Shaw was not consistent. Find the abbreviated words which *are* written with the apostrophe. What is the rule for using the apostrophe in abbreviations? Which other words are commonly abbreviated in dialogue?

Writing

Write an account of this story from the Centurion's point of view.

- Decide whether the Centurion would have more sympathy for Lentulus or Ferrovius. You could write the account as a diary entry, or perhaps as an article for the army newspaper, headlined 'Christian converts young Roman business-man.'

FAWLTY TOWERS: BASIL THE RAT

FROM A TELEVISION SCRIPT BY
JOHN CLEESE AND CONNIE BOOTH

Learning objectives

- to understand how a comic character is created
- to understand how script-writers use different kinds of humour

Discussion

- 'Farce' is the name given to comedy that includes exaggerated characters, coincidence, mistaken identity, embarrassment and narrow escapes. How many television series can you think of which include this kind of comedy?

THE STORY SO FAR

The hotel is being visited by a Health Inspector. Basil, the owner, rushes up to see Manuel, the Spanish waiter, in his room, to tell him to get the dead pigeons out of the water tank. Suddenly he notices a cage …

Basil:	*(noticing a cage containing a rodent, on the bedside cabinet)* What is that?
Manuel:	Is my hamster.
Basil:	… Hamster?
Manuel:	Si, Si.
Basil:	Manuel, that's a rat.
Manuel:	No, no, is hamster.
Basil:	Well, of course it's a rat! You have rats in Spain, don't you? – or did Franco have them all shot?
Manuel:	No, is hamster.
Basil:	Is rat.
Manuel:	No, I think so too.
Basil:	What?
Manuel:	I say to man in shop, 'Is rat.' He say, 'No, no, is special kind of hamster. Is Filigree Siberian hamster.' Only one in shop. He make special price, only five pound.
Basil:	*(calmly)* Have you ever heard of the bubonic plague,

	Manuel? It was very popular here at one time. A lot of pedigree hamsters came over on ships from Siberia … *(he takes the cage)*
Manuel:	What are you doing?
Basil:	I'm sorry, Manuel, this is a rat.
Manuel:	No, no, is hamster.
Basil:	Is not hamster. Hamsters are small and cuddly. Cuddle this, you'd never play the guitar again.

He walks out of the room with the cage. In the corridor, Manuel comes after him in pursuit.

Manuel:	Que? Where you go? Where you go? Where you take him?
Basil:	I'm sorry, Manuel, he's got to go.
Manuel:	Go? No!
Basil:	Yes.
Manuel:	No, no, he mine. He stay with me.
Basil:	Now, look! This is a hotel! The Health Inspector comes tomorrow. If he finds this, I …. closed down … no warning … closed down, Finito. You, out of work. Back to Barcelona.
Manuel:	He do no hurt. He in cage, he safe, please …

He hangs on to Basil's leg. Miss Tibbs and Miss Gatsby appear at the top of the stairs.

Basil:	Good morning, ladies.
Miss Gatsby:	What's the matter?
Manuel:	He take my hamster. Please, no, Mr Fawlty.
Miss Tibbs:	*(reproachfully)* Mr Fawlty!!
Manuel:	I love him, I love him.
Miss Tibbs:	How could you.
Basil:	Excuse me.
Manuel:	He take it from my room.
Miss Tibbs:	*(comforting Manuel)* Ah, there there …
Miss Gatsby:	Never mind, it'll be all right.
Miss Tibbs:	You can keep it in our room.
Miss Gatsby:	Yes. *(to Basil)* That's right – we'll keep it in our room, Mr Fawlty. We'll look after it.

Basil holds the cage out at them. They scream.

Misses Tibbs & Gatsby:	Aaah! A rat! A rat! A rat!! *(they scurry off)*
Manuel:	No, is Siberian hamster … filigree … *(but Basil has disappeared downstairs)*

In the kitchen, the cage is on the table. Basil and Sybil are discussing it.

Sybil:	Well, why didn't you check?
Basil:	What?

Sybil:	Well, you mean he's had it a whole year and you've only just found out?
Basil:	Yes.
Sybil:	Well, supposing the Health Inspector had seen it.
Basil:	I know.
Sybil:	He could have closed us down … Well, what you going to do with it, Basil? You can't keep it here.
Basil:	I know.
Sybil:	And don't let it loose in the garden, he'll come back in the house.
Basil:	I wasn't going to let it go in the garden.
Sybil:	Well, what you going to do with it?
Basil:	I don't know. I'll take it away, let it go. Give it its freedom.
Sybil:	You can't do that, Basil – he wouldn't be able to defend himself.
Basil:	He's a rat, isn't he?
Sybil:	He's domesticated *(to the rat)* aren't you?
Basil:	Well, you're domesticated. You do all right. Look, he's not going to get mugged by a gang of field-mice, is he?
Sybil:	Basil, he's Manuel's pet. We have duty to it … perhaps we could find a home for him.
Basil:	All right! I'll put an ad in the papers! Wanted, kind home for enormous savage rodent. Answers to the name of Sybil. Look, I'll take it out into the country, let him go…
Sybil:	No! I cannot abide cruelty to living creatures.
Basil:	Well, I'm a creature, you can abide it to me.
Sybil:	You're not living. *(Manuel comes in)* Look Manuel, we were just wondering what we ought to do …
Manuel:	Mrs Fawlty, please understand. If he go, I go.
Basil:	*(putting out his hand)* Well, goodbye.
Sybil:	*(to Manuel)* Please listen. You know we really can't keep him here. The Health Inspector wouldn't …
Manuel:	Mrs Fawlty. He here one year. He do no harm.
Sybil:	But, Manuel, listen … if they see your rat they could close the hotel down. *(to Basil)* Perhaps it would be simplest to have him put to S-L-E-E-P.
Basil:	Who, him or the rat? We might get a discount if we had 'em both done.
Manuel:	'Spleep'?
Polly:	*(coming in)* Manuel, I've rung my friend – it's all right – she'll take him.
Manuel:	Que?
Polly:	She has lots of animals, and it's not far away. You can go

and see him whenever you want. So come on, we'll take him over there now.

Manuel: But he forget me.

Basil: *(giving him the cage)* Well, rats are like that, Manuel. Don't get involved with 'em.

Polly: Come on, Manuel.

Sybil: I think it's the best solution, Manuel.

Polly: Oh, he'll be happy, you'll see.

Polly and Manuel leave the kitchen with the cage.

Sybil: Sad, isn't it.

Basil: Well … look at it from the point of view of the rat.

Sybil: What?

Basil: Would you want to spend the rest of your life with Manuel waiting on you?

Outside, Polly and Manuel walk down the drive with the cage between them.

Questions

Checking the facts

❶ What is Manuel keeping in the cage?

❷ How exactly was Manuel cheated by the pet-shop owner?

❸ What does 'filigree' mean? Which word is Manuel confusing it with?

❹ Why is Basil so desperate to get Manuel's 'pet' out of the hotel?

❺ What is the solution offered by Polly (the hotel assistant)?

 Explain what Basil says and does to get the rat out of the hotel, how Manuel argues to keep it, and what finally happens to it.

WRITE ABOUT

● the visit of the Health Inspector

● Basil's suggestions about what to do with the rat

● the discussion with Sybil

● Manuel's claims that it isn't a rat at all

● Polly's suggestion.

B *Basil Fawlty is one of the best-known of all television comic characters. What do we learn about him from this extract?*

COMMENT UPON

- his conversations with Manuel
- his reaction when he spots the rat
- his treatment of Miss Gatsby and Miss Tibbs
- his relationship with Sybil
- his wit.

 C *Which different kinds of humour are to be found in this extract?*

DISCUSS

- visual humour, things that make us laugh because of the way they look
- verbal humour, which depends on what people say and the way they say it
- witty or pointed comments from characters
- characters who are funny in themselves
- humour that comes from the situation and the complications that arise.

Grammar Spelling Punctuation

Standard English

Because Manuel is just learning English, he tends to abbreviate what he says, speaking the key words only: 'Is my hamster ... I say to man in shop ...'

- It is easy to understand what he says, but Standard English would require him to be clearer about a number of things, including tenses of verbs.

- What should the following be in standard English? Write out the correct versions and say whether the verbs are then in the present, past or future tense. (In some cases you have a choice.)

  'I say to man in shop.'   'He take it from my room.'

  'He make special price...'   'He here one year. He do no harm.'

  'Where you go? Where you take him?'   'But he forget me.'

  'He stay with me.'

Writing

Write a short story in which you have been told to get rid of something, but find a way of keeping it.

- You could include the arguments which take place when you are told it has to go; tell the story from your own point of view or someone else's; set it at home, school, or a place like the hotel in *Basil the Rat.*

JOURNEY'S END

FROM A STAGE PLAY BY R C SHERRIFF

Learning objectives

- to understand how a dramatist introduces new characters
- to understand how a dramatist establishes the setting and important background details

Discussion

- What do you know about the conditions of fighting in the Great War? Why was it known as 'trench warfare'? How did the men live when they were not fighting? What was a 'dug-out'?

THE STORY SO FAR

The play is set in the trenches in the final year of the Great War. Captain Hardy's company have come to the end of their six-day shift and are about to be relieved by another company which includes Captain Osborne …

Hardy:	*(looking round)* Hullo, Osborne! Your fellows arriving?
Osborne:	*(hitching off his pack and dropping it in a corner)* Yes. They're just coming in.
Hardy:	Splendid! Have a drink.
Osborne:	Thanks. *(He crosses and sits on the left-hand bed.)*
Hardy:	*(passing the whisky and a mug)* Don't have too much water. It's rather strong today.
Osborne:	*(slowly mixing a drink)* I wonder what it *is* they put in the water.
Hardy:	Some sort of disinfectant, I suppose.
Osborne:	I'd rather have the microbes, wouldn't you?
Hardy:	I would – yes –
Osborne:	Well, cheero.
Hardy:	Cheero. Excuse my sock, won't you?
Osborne:	Certainly. It's a nice-looking sock.
Hardy:	It is rather, isn't it? Guaranteed to keep the feet dry. Trouble is, it gets so wet doing it.

Osborne:	Stanhope asked me to come and take over. He's looking after the men coming in.
Hardy:	Splendid! You know, I'm awfully glad you've come.
Osborne:	I heard it was a quiet bit of line up here.
Hardy:	Well, yes – in a way. But you never know. Sometimes nothing happens for hours on end; then – all of a sudden – 'over she comes!' – rifle grenades – Minnies[1] – and those horrid little things like pineapples – you know.
Osborne:	I know.
Hardy:	Swish – swish – swish – swish – BANG!
Osborne:	All right – all right – I know.
Hardy:	They simply blew us to bits yesterday. Minnies – enormous ones; about twenty. Three bang in the trench. I really *am* glad you've come; I'm not simply being polite.
Osborne:	Do much damage?
Hardy:	Awful. A dug-out got blown up and came down in the men's tea. They were frightfully annoyed.
Osborne:	I know. There's nothing worse than dirt in your tea.
Hardy:	By the way, you know the big German attack's expected any day now?
Osborne:	It's been expected for the last month.
Hardy:	Yes, but it's very near now: there's funny things happening over in the Boche[2] country. I've been out listening at night when it's quiet. There's more transport than usual coming up – you can hear it rattling over the pavé[3] all night; more trains in the distance – puffing and going away again, one after another, bringing up loads and loads of men –
Osborne:	Yes. It's coming – pretty soon now.
Hardy:	Are you here for six days?
Osborne:	Yes.
Hardy:	Then I should think you get it – right in the neck.
Osborne:	Well, you won't be far away. Come along, let's do this handing over. Where's the map?
Hardy:	Here we are.

(He gropes among the papers on the table and finds a tattered map.)

	We hold about two hundred yards of front line. We've got a Lewis gun[4] just here – and one here, in this little sap[5]. Sentry posts where the crosses are –
Osborne:	Where do the men sleep?
Hardy:	I don't know. The sergeant-major sees to that. *(He points off to the left.)* The servants and signallers sleep in there. Two

[1] *mine-throwers*

[2] *German*

[3] *stone cobbled road*

[4] *machine gun*
[5] *narrow trench projecting towards enemy lines*

officers in here, and three in there. *(He points to the right-hand tunnel.)* That is, if you've *got* five officers.

Osborne: We've only got four at present, but a new man's coming up tonight. He arrived at transport lines a day or two ago.

Hardy: I hope you get better luck than I did with *my* last officer. He got lumbago the first night and went home. Now he's got a job lecturing young officers on 'Life in the Front Line.'

Osborne: Yes. They do send some funny people over here nowadays. I hope we're lucky and get a youngster straight from school. They're the kind that do best.

Hardy: I suppose they are, really.

Osborne: Five beds, you say? *(He examines the one he is sitting on.)* Is this the best one?

Hardy: Oh, no. *(He points to the bed in the right corner.)* *That's* mine. The ones in the other dug-out haven't got any bottoms to them. You keep yourself in by hanging your arms and legs over the sides. Mustn't hang your legs too low, or the rats gnaw your boots.

Osborne: You got many rats here?

Hardy: I should say – roughly – about two million; but then, of course, I don't see them all. *(He begins to put on his sock and draw on his boot.)*

Questions

Checking the facts

❶ What is Hardy's response to Osborne's suggestion that this is a quiet part of the line?

❷ What damage was done when three 'Minnies' landed in the trench?

❸ What evidence do they have that the German 'big attack' is coming soon?

❹ How many officers usually sleep in each dugout?

❺ What happened to the last new officer?

What does this extract reveal about the war at this time?

WRITE ABOUT

- the weapons used by the Germans
- the previous day's attack
- the German preparation for the big attack
- living conditions in the trenches.

 What do we learn about the character of Captain Hardy?

COMMENT UPON

- his attitude towards things such as army socks, the different weapons used by the Germans, the attack of the day before, the last new officer to arrive
- his views about the big attack
- his reaction to Osborne's questions about the map and sleeping arrangements.

 In what ways does the dialogue help to set the scene and establish the atmosphere?

DISCUSS

- the details about living conditions
- the use of the technical terms of warfare
- the references to the imminent big attack.

Grammar Spelling Punctuation

The changing language

One of the most interesting features of language is the way it constantly changes.

- Words and expressions which are popular one year can become unfashionable the next. Hardy and Osborne use several expressions not heard much any more.

- Discuss in pairs what people would say today instead of:
  'Cheero.'   'horrid'
  'Splendid!'   'They were frightfully annoyed.'
  'I'm awfully glad …'

Writing

Write the script for a scene in which Osborne reports his meeting with Hardy to a senior officer.

- Include references to the recent attack on the trenches and Hardy's information about the German troop movements. Osborne might also express opinions about Hardy as a company commander.

THE PIED PIPER OF HAMELIN

FROM A POEM BY ROBERT BROWNING

Learning objectives

- to understand how a pre-1900 narrative poem is presented

- to understand how a poet uses rhyme and rhythm to describe people and place

Discussion

- Which stories do you know in which somebody makes a bargain and then tries to get out of it?

The Pied Piper of Hamelin

Hamelin Town's in Brunswick,
By famous Hanover city;
 The river Weser, deep and wide,
 Washes its wall on the southern side;
 A pleasanter spot you never spied;
But, when begins my ditty,
 Almost five hundred years ago,
 To see the townsfolk suffer so
 From vermin, was a pity.

II

 Rats!
They fought the dogs, and killed the cats,
 And bit the babies in the cradles,
 And ate the cheeses out of the vats,
And licked the soup from the cooks' own ladles,
Split open the kegs of salted sprats,
Made nests inside men's Sunday hats,
And even spoiled the women's chats,
 By drowning their speaking

With shrieking and squeaking
In fifty different sharps and flats.

III

At last the people in a body
   To the Town Hall came flocking:
''Tis clear,' cried they 'our Mayor's a noddy;
   And as for our Corporation—shocking
To think we buy gowns lined with ermine
For dolts that can't or won't determine
What's best to rid us of our vermin!
You hope, because you're old and obese,
To find in the furry civic robe ease?
Rouse up, Sirs! Give your brains a racking
To find the remedy we're lacking,
Or, sure as fate, we'll send you packing!'
At this the Mayor and Corporation
Quaked with a mighty consternation.

IV

An hour they sate in council,
   At length the Mayor broke silence:
'For a guilder I'd my ermine gown sell;
   I wish I were a mile hence!
It's easy to bid one rack one's brain—
I'm sure my poor head aches again
I've scratched it so, and all in vain.
Oh for a trap, a trap, a trap!'
Just as he said this, what should hap
At the chamber door but a gentle tap?
'Bless us,' cried the Mayor, 'what's that?'
'Anything like the sound of a rat
Makes my heart go pit-a-pat!'

V

'Come in!'—the Mayor cried, looking bigger:
And in did come the strangest figure!
His queer long coat from heel to head
Was half of yellow and half of red;
And he himself was tall and thin,
With sharp blue eyes, each like a pin,
And light loose hair, yet swarthy skin,
No tuft on cheek nor beard on chin,

But lips where smiles went out and in—
There was no guessing his kith and kin!
And nobody could enough admire
The tall man and his quaint attire.

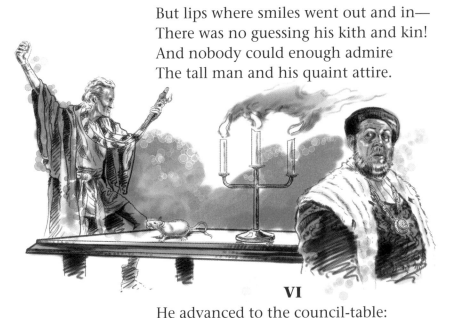

VI

He advanced to the council-table:
And, 'Please your honours,' said he, 'I'm able,
By means of a secret charm, to draw
All creatures living beneath the sun,
That creep or swim or fly or run,
After me so as you never saw!
And I chiefly use my charm
On creatures that do people harm,
The mole and toad and newt and viper;
And people call me the Pied Piper.'
(And here they noticed round his neck
A scarf of red and yellow stripe,
To match with his coat of the self-same cheque;
And at the scarf's end hung a pipe;
And his fingers, they noticed, were ever straying
As if impatient to be playing
Upon this pipe, as low it dangled
Over his vesture so old-fangled.)
'Yet,' said he, 'poor piper as I am,
In Tartary I freed the Cham,[1]
Last June, from his huge swarms of gnats;
I eased in Asia the Nizam[1]
Of a monstrous brood of vampyre bats:
And as for what your brain bewilders,
If I can rid your town of rats
Will you give me a thousand guilders?'
'One? fifty thousand!'—was the exclamation
Of the astonished Mayor and Corporation.

[1] *Great leaders in other parts of the world*

VII

Into the street the Piper stept,
    Smiling first a little smile,
As if he knew what magic slept
    In his quiet pipe the while;
Then, like a musical adept,
To blow the pipe his lips he wrinkled,
And green and blue his sharp eyes twinkled
Like a candle-flame where salt is sprinkled;
And ere three shrill notes the pipe uttered,
You heard as if an army muttered;
And the muttering grew to a grumbling;
And the grumbling grew to a mighty rumbling;
And out of the houses the rats came tumbling.
Great rats, small rats, lean rats, brawny rats,
Brown rats, black rats, grey rats, tawny rats,
Grave old plodders, gay young friskers,
    Fathers, mothers, uncles, cousins,
Cocking tails and pricking whiskers,
    Families by tens and dozens,
Brothers, sisters, husbands, wives—
Followed the Piper for their lives.
From street to street he piped advancing,
And step for step they followed dancing,
Until they came to the river Weser
Wherein all plunged and perished!

Robert Browning

Questions

Checking the facts

❶ On which bank of the River Weser is Hamelin?

❷ Why are the people of Hamelin angry with the Mayor?

❸ What is meant in verse five by the phrase 'There was no guessing his kith and kin'?

❹ Why does the Pied Piper offer his services to Hamelin?

❺ How has the Pied Paper got his name?

What picture do you have of the town of Hamelin?

WRITE ABOUT

- its location
- the townsfolk
- the Mayor and Corporation
- what the rats are doing in the houses and streets.

 How does the Pied Piper 'sell himself' to the people of Hamelin?

COMMENT UPON

- his appearance
- his offer of help
- his claims of past success with vermin
- the magic of his pipe.

 'The Pied Piper of Hamelin' is a famous narrative poem. Judging from this extract, why do you think it has become so popular?

DISCUSS

- its subject matter
- the poet's description of the Pied Piper and the rats
- the poem's rhythms and rhymes
- your own response to the poem and the story it tells.

Grammar Spelling Punctuation

Revising apostrophes

Divide the following words into two lists, according to whether the apostrophe is being used for a) abbreviation, b) possession.

- For each word in list a), write out the full version. For each word in list b), explain the position of the apostrophe according to the rule.

Town's	cooks'	men's	women's	'Tis	Mayor's	can't
won't	What's	you're	we're	It's	one's	I'm

Writing

Legend has it that in 1284 Hamelin was infested with rats and a mysterious piper appeared.

- Imagine you lived in the town at that time. Write a diary account of events: the plague and what followed. Use the poem as a starting point and develop your own ideas.

'POEM FOR MY SISTER' AND 'SISTERS'

POEMS BY LIZ LOCHHEAD AND WENDY COPE

Learning objectives

- to understand how two poets treat a similar subject
- to understand how poems are written

Discussion

- Which stories do you know which feature friendships between brothers and sisters? What is it that helps them to stay friends?

Poem for My Sister

My little sister likes to try my shoes,
to strut in them,
admire her spindle-thin twelve-year-old legs
in this season's styles.
She says they fit perfectly,
but wobbles
on their high heels, they're
hard to balance.

I like to watch my little sister
playing hopscotch, admire the
   neat hops-and-skips of her,
their quick peck,
never-missing their mark, not
over-stepping the line.
She is competent at peever.[1]

I try to warn my little sister
about unsuitable shoes,

[1] Hopscotch

2 *Hard patches of skin on the foot*

point out my own distorted feet, the calluses,[2]
odd patches of hard skin.
I should not like to see her
in my shoes.
I wish she would stay
sure footed,
        sensibly shod.

Liz Lochhead

Sisters (for Marian)

My sister
was the bad one –
said what she thought
and did what she liked
and didn't care.

At ten she wore
a knife tucked in
her leather belt,
dreamed of *being*
a prince on a white horse.

Became a dolly bird
with dyed hair longer
than her skirts, pulling
the best of the local talent.
Mother wept and prayed.

At thirty she's divorced,
has cropped her locks
and squats in Hackney –
tells me 'God created man
then realised Her mistake.'

I'm not like her,
I'm good – but now
I'm working on it.
Fighting through
to my own brand of badness.

I am glad of her
at last – her conferences,
her anger, and her boots.
We talk and smoke
and laugh at everybody –

two bad sisters.

Wendy Cope

Questions

Checking the facts

Poem for My Sister
❶ Why does little sister want to wear shoes that don't fit her?
❷ Why does the poet enjoy watching her sister play hopscotch?
Sisters
❸ In what ways was the sister 'bad'?
❹ How did the mother respond to Marian's behaviour?
❺ What does the poet mean by 'I'm working on it' (line 23)?

What does each poet admire in her sister?

WRITE ABOUT

- childhood scenes
- their innocence
- the loss of innocence
- being a sister.

 In what ways are the two poems similar and different in subject matter?

COMMENT UPON

- the time-frame of each poem
- sisterly attitudes
- hopes and ambitions
- the tone of the poems, and your response to them.

 Poet Gillian Clarke has said that 'poetry is not chopped up prose'. Another writer once said that 'poetry equals the best words in the best order'. How are these poems constructed?

DISCUSS

- how the poets compress language for a particular effect
- the different meanings some words can have
- 'snapshot' images they use
- where they place particular words
- where lines end; line and verse length.

Grammar Spelling Punctuation

Hyphens and dashes

Look at each poet's use of hyphens and dashes in the two poems.

- Where is each used, and what is it used for?

- Write down your own 'rules' for the use of the hyphen and dash, based on these poems.

Writing

You probably have vivid memories of certain events and incidents in your childhood involving sisters and brothers, step-family or a friend's family.

- Describe one event in a poem or short prose passage of your own. If there was a lesson learned by anyone, try to include it in your piece of writing. You could also add some cartoons!

'A CASE OF MURDER' AND 'THE SECRET IN THE CAT'

POEMS BY
VERNON SCANNELL AND MAY SWENSON

Learning objectives

- to understand how two poets write about an animal

- to understand how poets use literal and figurative language

Discussion

- 'Animal Rights' is a subject much talked about. What 'rights' do you think animals have? Are they the same as or different from human rights?

A Case of Murder

They should not have left him there alone,
Alone that is except for the cat.
He was only nine, not old enough
To be left alone in a basement flat,
Alone, that is, except for the cat.
A dog would have been a different thing,
A big gruff dog with slashing jaws,
But a cat with round eyes mad as gold,
Plump as a cushion with tucked-in paws—
Better have left him with a fair-sized rat!
But what they did was leave him with a cat.
He hated that cat; he watched it sit,
A buzzing machine of soft black stuff,
He sat and watched and he hated it,
Snug in its fur, hot blood in a muff,
And its mad gold stare and the way it sat

Crooning dark warmth: he loathed all that.
So he took Daddy's stick and he hit the cat.
Then quick as a sudden crack in glass
It hissed, black flash, to a hiding place
In the dust and dark beneath the couch,
And he followed the grin on his new-made face,
A wide-eyed, frightened snarl of a grin,
And he took the stick and he thrust it in,
Hard and quick in the furry dark,
The black fur squealed and he felt his skin
Prickle with sparks of dry delight.
Then the cat again came into sight,
Shot for the door that wasn't quite shut,
But the boy, quick too, slammed fast the door:
The cat, half-through, was cracked like a nut
And the soft black thud was dumped on the floor.
Then the boy was suddenly terrified
And he bit his knuckles and cried and cried;
But he had to do something with the dead
   thing there.
His eyes squeezed beads of salty prayer
But the wound of fear gaped wide and raw;
He dared not touch the thing with his hands
So he fetched a spade and shovelled it
And dumped the load of heavy fur
In the spidery cupboard under the stair
Where it's been for years, and though it died
It's grown in that cupboard and its hot low purr
Grows slowly louder year by year:
There'll not be a corner for the boy to hide
When the cupboard swells and all sides split
And the huge black cat pads out of it.

Vernon Scannell

The Secret in the Cat

I took my cat apart
to see what made him purr.
Like an electric clock
or like the snore

of a warming kettle,
something fizzled and sizzled in him.
Was he a soft car,
the engine bubbling sound?

Was there a wire beneath his fur,
or humming throttle?
I undid his throat.
Within was no stir.

I opened up his chest
as though it were a door:
no whisk or rattle there.
I lifted off his skull:

no hiss or murmur.
I halved his little belly
but found no gear,
no cause for static.

So I replaced his lid,
laced his little gut.
His heart into his vest I slid
and buttoned up his throat.

His tail rose to a rod
and beckoned to the air.
Some voltage made him vibrate
warmer than before.

Whiskers and a tail:
perhaps they caught
some radar code
emitted as a pip, a dot-and-dash

of woollen sound.
My car a kind of tuning fork? –
amplifier? – telegraph? –
doing secret signal work?

His eyes elliptic tubes:
there's a message in his stare.
I stroke him
but cannot find the dial.

May Swenson

Questions

Checking the facts

A Case of Murder

❶ Who are 'they' in line one?

❷ List three things about the cat which the boy hates.

❸ What do you understand (five lines from the end) by the phrase
   'It's grown in that cupboard'?

The Secret in the Cat

❹ What is the poet actually doing in the first two lines?

❺ Where is the half-way point in the poem?
   What is the poet's conclusion about the cat she is describing?

What picture of the cat is given in 'A Case of Murder'?

WRITE ABOUT

- its physical appearance
- its movements
- how the boy reacts to it
- how the cat looks when it's dead.

 What is special about a cat according to May Swenson in 'The Secret in the Cat'?

COMMENT UPON

- the cat's appearance
- its movements
- how humans see and think about it
- its secrets.

 What do the two poems have in common and in what way are they different?

DISCUSS

- the subject matter
- *why* you think the poems were written: think about 'A Case of Murder' in particular
- the vocabulary and images used to describe the cats
- your own response to the ideas in the poems.

Grammar Spelling Punctuation

Revising figurative language

Write down six phrases from the poems where the poets are using figurative language about cats. For example: 'a buzzing machine' 'the engine bubbling sound'.

- Discuss with a partner the images and pictures of cats that the poets are trying to create for the reader. Make a few drawings to help you with this.

Writing

Think of an animal whose appearance, moods and movements you are familiar with – perhaps a pet or an animal you see regularly in your garden or local area.

- Write a poem – in the style of May Swenson – about it.
  Title: 'The Secret in the …'

'CATCHING CRABS' AND 'PRAISE SONG FOR MY MOTHER'

POEMS BY

DAVID DABYDEEN AND GRACE NICHOLS

Learning objectives

- to understand how poets write about their childhoods
- to understand how poets use language to describe people and places

Discussion

- Imagine yourself in twenty years' time living in another country. What would your strongest memories be of where you live now?

Catching Crabs

Ruby and me stalking savannah
Crab season with cutlass and sack like big folk.
Hiding behind stones or clumps of bush
Crabs locked knee-deep in mud mating
And Ruby seven years old feeling strange at the sex
And me horrified to pick them up
Plunge them into the darkness of bag,
So all day we scout to catch the lonesome ones
Who don't mind cooking because they got no prospect
Of family, and squelching through the mud,
Cutlass clearing bush at our feet,
We come home tired slow, weighed down with plenty
Which Ma throw live into boiling pot piece-piece.
Tonight we'll have one big happy curry feed.
We'll test out who teeth and jaw strongest
Who will grow up to be the biggest

Or who will make most terrible cannibal.
We leave behind a mess of bones and shell
And come to England and America
Where Ruby hustles in a New York tenement
And me writing poetry at Cambridge,
Death long catch Ma, the house boarded up
Breeding wasps, woodlice in its dark-sack belly:
I am afraid to walk through weed yard,
Reach the door, prise open, look,
In case the pot still bubbles magical
On the fireside, and I see Ma
Working a ladle, slow-
Limbed, crustacean[1]-old, alone,
In case the woodsmoke and curry steam
Burn my child-eye and make it cry.

[1] *Like a crab*

David Dabydeen

Praise Song for My Mother

You were
water to me
deep and bold and fathoming

You were
moon's eye to me
pull and grained and mantling

You were
sunrise to me
rise and warm and streaming

You were
the fishes red gill to me
the flame tree's spread to me
the crab's leg/the fried plantain smell
            replenishing replenishing

Go to your wide futures, you said.

Grace Nichols

Questions

Checking the facts

Catching Crabs

❶ What are the children doing in verse one?

❷ Where are the poet and his sister in verse two?

Praise Song for My Mother

❸ Who are the 'You' and 'me' in this poem?

❹ What is meant by the last line of the poem?

 **Both poets are remembering their childhoods in Guyana and in the Caribbean.**

WRITE ABOUT

● where they lived

● what they ate

● what they did as children.

 **In what ways are the two poems similar and different?**

COMMENT UPON

● the people in the poems

● memories of the Caribbean

● the 'voice' of each poem

● how each poem ends.

 **Why do you think David Dabydeen and Grace Nichols wrote these poems?**

DISCUSS

● the importance of their mothers in their lives

● the fact that each has moved away from the Caribbean

● the way they describe their native Guyana

● your own response to the poems.

Grammar Spelling Punctuation

Make a list of the words and phrases which give you a sense of the Caribbean.

● Include examples of Caribbean dialect in 'Catching Crabs'.

Writing

Write a poem or short story of your own in which you return – many years from now – to a place from your childhood.

● Try to capture memories of people and places in your writing.

THE CHARGE OF THE LIGHT BRIGADE

A POEM BY ALFRED LORD TENNYSON

Learning objectives

- to understand how a pre-twentieth century narrative poem is written
- to understand how style and subject matter are matched in a poem

Discussion

- In war, should soldiers in the field of battle always obey orders? Are there any times when orders could be ignored?

The Charge of the Light Brigade

I

Half a league, half a league,
  Half a league onward,
All in the valley of Death
  Rode the six hundred.
'Forward, the Light Brigade!
Charge for the guns!' he said;
Into the valley of Death
  Rode the six hundred.

II

'Forward, the Light Brigade!'
Was there a man dismay'd?
Not tho' the soldier knew
  Some one had blunder'd:
Their's not to make reply,
Their's not to reason why,
Their's but to do and die:
Into the valley of Death
  Rode the six hundred.

III

Cannon to right of them,
Cannon to left of them,
Cannon in front of them
  Volley'd and thunder'd;
Storm'd at with shot and
shell,
Boldly they rode and well,
Into the jaws of Death,
Into the mouth of Hell
  Rode the six hundred.

IV

Flash'd all their sabres bare,
Flash'd as they turn'd in air,
Sabring the gunners there,
Charging an army, while
  All the world wonder'd:
Plunged in the battery-smoke
Right thro' the line they broke;
Cossack and Russian
Reel'd from the sabre-stroke

Shatter'd and sunder'd.
Then they rode back, but not,
   Not the six hundred.

Back from the mouth of Hell,
All that was left of them,
   Left of six hundred.

V

Cannon to right of them,
Cannon to left of them,
Cannon behind them
   Volley'd and thunder'd;
Storm'd at with shot and shell,
While horse and hero fell,
They that had fought so well
Came thro' the jaws of Death

VI

When can their glory fade?
O the wild charge they made!
   All the world wonder'd.
Honour the charge they made!
Honour the Light Brigade,
   Noble six hundred!

Alfred Lord Tennyson

Questions

Checking the facts

❶ What is the Light Brigade?

❷ What is hinted at in line 12, 'Some one had blunder'd'?

❸ Who is fighting whom in stanza IV?

❹ What are the main weapons being used in this battle?

❺ How many soldiers survived the battle, do you think?

How does the poet match his style to the content of the poem?

DISCUSS

- the structure of the six stanzas and their length
- the poem's rhyming scheme and internal rhythms
- the choice of vocabulary and repetition of certain phrases
- the use of punctuation.

 Describe the 'Charge of the Light Brigade'.

WRITE ABOUT

- the soldiers
- the battlefield setting
- the various 'jaws of Death'
- the return of the soldiers.

 What ideas run through the poem?

COMMENT UPON

- the plan of attack and its execution
- the state of mind of the soldiers
- the poet's attitude towards the soldiers and the battle
- the poet's comments on glory and death.

Grammar Spelling Punctuation

Prepositions

The poem makes good use of several key prepositions.

- Note down all those you can find and compare your list with a partner.

- Discuss in what way the prepositions are important to the shape of the poem.

- Look at the sketch of the scene on the battlefield. Where are different groups of soldiers positioned in relation to one another?

Writing

Write your own poem about soldier-to-soldier battle.

- You could do this based on the Tennyson poem by using the following lines as a kind of refrain:

      'Cannon to right of them
      Cannon to left of them
      Cannon in front of them.'

'A CRABBIT OLD WOMAN' AND 'FOR MY GRANDMOTHER KNITTING'

POEMS BY PHYLLIS MCCORMACK AND LIZ LOCHHEAD

Learning objectives

- to understand how two poets write about the same subject
- to understand how poets use contrasting 'voices' in their poems

Discussion

- When you hear the word 'old', what words spring to mind?
- Do you think that society treats older people well?

A Crabbit Old Woman

What do you see, nurses,
what do you see?
Are you thinking
when you're looking at me,
A crabbit old woman,
not very wise,
Uncertain of habit,
with far-away eyes,
Who dribbles her food
and makes no reply,
When you say in a loud voice,
'I do wish you'd try,'
Who seems not to notice
the things that you do,
And forever is losing
a stocking or shoe,
Who, quite unresisting,
lets you do as you will,
With bathing and feeding,
the long day to fill?
Is that what you're thinking,
is that what you see?
Then open your eyes,
you're not looking at me.
I'll tell you who I am
as I sit here so still,
As I move at your bidding,
as I eat at your will,
I'm a small child of ten
with a father and mother,
Brothers and sisters,

who love one another;
A young girl of sixteen
with wings on her feet,
Dreaming that soon
a true lover she'll meet;
A bride now at twenty –
my heart gives a leap,
Remembering the vows
that I promised to keep;
At twenty-five now
I have young of my own,
Who need me to build
a secure, happy home;
A woman of thirty,
my young now grow fast,
Bound to each other
with ties that should last;
At forty my young sons
will soon all be gone,
But my man stays beside me
to see I don't mourn;
At fifty once more
babies play round my knee,
Again we know children,
my loved one and me.
Dark days are upon me,
my husband is dead,
I look at the future,
I shudder with dread,
For my young are all busy
with young of their own,
And I think of the years
and the love I have known.
I'm an old woman now
and nature is cruel,
'Tis her jest to make
old age look like a fool.
The body it crumbles,
grace and vigour depart,
There now is a stone

where I once had a heart.
But inside this old carcass
a young girl still dwells,
And now and again
my battered heart swells.
I remember the joys,
I remember the pain,
And I'm loving and living
life over again.

I think of the years
all too few – gone too fast,
And accept the stark fact
that nothing can last.
So open your eyes, nurses,
open and see,
Not a crabbit old woman,
look closer – see ME.

Phyllis McCormack

For My Grandmother Knitting

There is no need they say but the needles still move
their rhythms in the working of your hands
as easily
as if your hands
were once again those sure and skilful hands
of the fisher-girl.

You are old now
and your grasp of things is not so good
but master of your movements then
deft and swift
you slit the still-ticking quick silver fish.
Hard work it was too
of necessity.

But now they say there is no need
as the needles move
in the working of your hands
once the hands of the bride
with the hand-span waist
once the hands of the miner's wife
who scrubbed his back
in a tin bath by the coal fire
once the hands of the mother
of six who made do and mended
scraped and slaved slapped sometimes
when necessary.

But now they say there is no need
the kids they say grandma
have too much already
more than they can wear
too many scarves and cardigans –
gran you do too much
there's no necessity.

At your window you wave
them goodbye Sunday.
With your painful hands
big on shrunken wrists.
Swollen-jointed. Red. Arthritic. Old.
But the needles still move
their rhythms in the working of your hands
easily
as if your hands remembered
of their own accord the pattern
as if your hands had forgotten
how to stop.

Liz Lochhead

Questions

Checking the facts

A Crabbit Old Woman

❶ What is the setting for this poem?

❷ How many generations are described?

❸ What does the poet most want from the nurses around her?

For My Grandmother Knitting

❹ Who are 'they', as mentioned in line 1?

❺ What work did the grandmother do as a young woman?

❻ What picture emerges of her married life?

What experiences have been shared by the two old women in these poems?

WRITE ABOUT

- their childhoods
- their family lives
- the attitude of the younger generation towards them
- their current state of mind and everyday activities.

 What is your picture of the old women described?

COMMENT UPON

- how they see themselves
- how others see them
- the descriptions of their physical appearances
- what your reactions to them in real life might be.

 Think about the style and 'voice' of each of the poems.

DISCUSS

- the first-person narrator in 'A Crabbit Old Woman'
- the second-person address in 'For My Grandmother Knitting'
- the tone and verse-form of the writing
- the closing lines of the poems.

Grammar Spelling Punctuation

Poetry and prose

What would these poems lose or gain if they were written in prose rather than as poems?

- Rewrite each as a short piece of prose description.

- With a partner, talk about how prose and poetry work in different ways and make us see the same subject a little differently.

Writing

Imagine one of the nurses reading 'A Crabbit Old Woman' and then responding to the poet's question: 'What do you see?'

- Write a short letter or poem titled 'A Nurse's Reply'.

Imagine Liz Lochhead's grandmother writing a letter or poem back to the poet, after she had read 'For My Grandmother Knitting'.

- What might she say?

'HURRICANE' AND 'WIND'

POEMS BY JAMES BERRY AND TED HUGHES

Learning objectives

- to understand how two poets treat similar subject matter

- to understand how to compare writing from different cultures

Discussion

- Have you ever experienced violent winds or storms and been caught up in their power? What were your feelings at the time? What words come to mind to describe the scene?

Hurricane

Under the low black clouds
the wind was all
speedy feet, all horns and breath,
all bangs, howls, rattles,
in every hen house,
church hall and school.

Roaring, screaming, returning,
it made forced entry, shoved walls,
made rifts, brought roofs down,
hitting rooms to sticks apart.

It wrung soft banana trees,
broke tough trunks of palms.
It pounded vines of yams,
left fields battered up.

Invisible with such ecstasy –
with no intervention of sun or man –
everywhere kept changing branches.

Zinc sheets are kites.
Leaves are panic swarms.
Fowls are fixed with feathers turned.
Goats, dogs, pigs,
all are people together.

Then growling it slunk away
from muddy, mossy trail and boats
in hedges: and cows, ratbats, trees,
fish, all dead in the road.

James Berry

Wind

This house has been far out at sea all night,
The woods crashing through darkness, the booming hills,
Winds stampeding the fields under the window
Floundering black astride and blinding wet

Till day rose; then under an orange sky
The hills had new places, and wind wielded
Blade-light, luminous black and emerald,
Flexing like the lens of a mad eye.

At noon I scaled along the house-side as far as
The coal-house door. I dared once to look up—
Through the brunt wind that dented the balls of my eyes
The tent of the hills drummed and strained its guyrope,

The fields quivering, the skyline a grimace,
At any second to bang and vanish with a flap:
The wind flung a magpie away and a black—
Back gull bent like an iron bar slowly. The house

Rang like some fine green goblet in the note
That any second would shatter it. Now deep
In chairs, in front of the great fire, we grip
Our hearts and cannot entertain book, thought,

Or each other. We watch the fire blazing,
And feel the roots of the house move, but sit on,
Seeing the window tremble to come in,
Hearing the stones cry out under the horizons.

Ted Hughes

Questions

Checking the facts

Hurricane
❶ Which country do you think this poem is set in?
❷ How does the hurricane end?
Wind
❸ Where is this poem set?
❹ Which birds feature in the poem?
❺ What are the thoughts of those inside the house?

What do the two poems have in common?

WRITE ABOUT

- what happens in each poem
- the impact of the wind on the natural landscape
- the impact of the wind on buildings
- the wind's effect on animals and humans.

 In what ways are the two poems different in style and content?

COMMENT UPON

- their contrasting locations
- how the poems end
- their rhyming schemes and internal rhythms
- the poets' physical involvement in what they are seeing.

 How does each poet use literal and figurative language to powerful effect?

DISCUSS

- straight, accurate description of the landscape
- use of alliteration
- use of onomatopoeic verbs
- use of simile and metaphor.

Grammar Spelling Punctuation

Verb tenses

Look at the use of verb tenses in each of the poems.

- Make two lists – under the headings PAST TENSE and PRESENT TENSE – of all the verbs James Berry and Ted Hughes include.

- Discuss with a partner why they choose to use different verb tenses at different points in the poems.

Writing

The best descriptive writing appeals to many of the five senses at the same time.

- Write a series of phrases which capture the mood and atmosphere of being alone in a violently windswept environment. This could be by the sea, or in city or country. Now link your phrases together to form the draft of a poem, with or without lines rhyming. Compare your lines with a partner's – combine the best phrases of each to produce a final version.

IF

A POEM BY RUDYARD KIPLING

Learning objectives

- to understand how a poet chooses particular vocabulary
- to understand how a poet structures verse

Discussion

- If you were giving advice to an elder sister or brother leaving home for the first time – and trusting they might listen to you – what five key points would you say to them?

If

If you can keep your head when all about you
    Are losing theirs and blaming it on you,
If you can trust yourself when all men doubt you,
    But make allowance for their doubting too;

If you can wait and not be tired by waiting,
    Or being lied about, don't deal in lies,
Or being hated, don't give way to hating,
    And yet don't look too good, nor talk too wise:

If you can dream – and not make dreams your master;
    If you can think – and not make thoughts your aim;
If you can meet with Triumph and Disaster
    And treat those two impostors just the same;
If you can bear to hear the truth you've spoken
    Twisted by knaves to make a trap for fools,
Or watch the things you gave your life to, broken,
    And stoop and build 'em up with worn-out tools:

If you can make one heap of all your winnings
    And risk it on one turn of pitch-and-toss,
And lose, and start again at your beginnings
    And never breathe a word about your loss;
If you can force your heart and nerve and sinew
    To serve your turn long after they are gone,
And so hold on when there is nothing in you
    Except the Will which says to them: 'Hold on!'

If you can talk with crowds and keep your virtue,
    Or walk with Kings – nor lose the common touch,
If neither foes nor loving friends can hurt you,
    If all men count with you, but none too much;
If you can fill the unforgiving minute
    With sixty seconds' worth of distance run,
Yours is the Earth and everything that's in it,
    And – which is more – you'll be a Man, my son!

Rudyard Kipling

Questions

Checking the facts

❶ In verse one, what does the poet say about 'trust' and 'hate'?

❷ In lines 11–12, why are 'Triumph and Disaster' called 'impostors' by the poet?

❸ What does verse three have to say about gambling?

❹ To whom is the poem written, do you think?

A *Reread these five pieces of advice offered in the poem, and explain them in your own words*

WRITE ABOUT

- blame and trust
- lying and hating
- beliefs and truths
- losing and winning
- values and friendship.

 B *How successful is 'If' as an 'advice poem' in your opinion?*

COMMENT UPON

- whether you would write about the same qualities that Kipling does
- what, for you, are the important moments in the poem
- which lines you think are particularly true
- what qualities or advice has been missed out
- your response to the final two lines.

 C *Rudyard Kipling's poem 'If' has repeatedly been voted one of the nation's favourite poems. Why do you think this is?*

DISCUSS

- the poem's structure and lay-out
- the rhyming scheme and images
- its timeless qualities
- other aspects of the poem that may appeal to people.

Grammar Spelling Punctuation

Working with a partner, discuss which lines of the poem refer to the following.

- All are abstract nouns. Use a dictionary and thesaurus to help you.

confidence	perseverance	sensitivity	determination
tolerance	honesty	modesty	level-headedness
patience	adventurousness	idealism	reliability
self-awareness	courage	open-mindedness	realism

Writing

Imagine you are a father or mother writing a letter to your teenage child.

- You want to offer advice about the world but you don't want to sound too stuffy and boring! Draft this out as a letter or poem. Compare your first drafts with a partner, and talk about ways in which they can be improved.

THE WARRINGTON BOMBINGS

FROM A BOOK BY KEITH GREENBERG

Learning objectives

- to understand how personal details can add to the impact of factual writing
- to understand how an opening chapter can introduce its subject

Discussion

- As a class, discuss what you know about terrorism. Why do people become terrorists? In particular, what do you know about the IRA?

SETTING THE SCENE

This extract from a book called Terrorism: Northern Ireland & Beyond.

It is March 1992 on a busy Saturday in Warrington, a town in the northwest of England. The shops are full and people are milling about in the streets. In the Parry household, Colin and Wendy Parry go off to the nearby city of Manchester to get Wendy's car serviced. Their son, Tim, is restless. Five weeks earlier he had his appendix removed, and there is still another week to go before the doctor will allow him to join in school sports. Tim Parry is big for a 12-year-old, and dead keen on sport. He has a few pounds, not enough for a pair of proper Everton goalie shorts, but possibly enough for an ordinary pair. He calls his friends. They have the afternoon to themselves, and looking is nearly as much fun as buying.

What sort of boy was Tim? His father would later say that he was a jester. He was the sort who would take a frog out of his pocket and wave it in front of you. He was like his Dad, big and physical, sporting and fun. His Mum and Dad worried that he wasn't doing well at school. He was bored because he was the oldest boy in his class, and maybe he felt he was getting left behind as boys just a month older than him moved on. Tim would be dead by the time his school report arrived. It would be a good report and his parents would know then that they needn't have worried at all about Tim's schoolwork.

Colin Parry's real worry, if only he knew it, should have been about a group of Irish Republican Army (IRA) terrorists who were spreading increasing havoc in the north of England. The IRA have carried out bombing and shooting attacks in Northern Ireland for more than 20 years, and they have frequently sent groups, which they called Active Service Units, to England. These units have bombed streets in London and murdered politicians who have spoken against them or their goal, a united Ireland. But no one expected the IRA to strike in Warrington.

Tim Parry hears the first bomb go off as he walks out of a shop. All around people are screaming and running. He runs too, but he runs towards the second bomb. It is sitting in a wastebin. Sixty-two seconds after the first bomb, the second one explodes. The blast shatters the bin's iron casing and flings chunks of metal across the street into the people running away. Tim is down, lying on the ground. His clothes are in tatters and he is bleeding. Another boy, three-year-old Jonathan Ball, is dead.

Usually, the IRA give warnings before their bombings, though these are often confused and too late for a full evacuation of the area. They devise a code to authenticate their warnings, and tell the police in advance what the next code will be. The police notify newspapers, radio stations and the Samaritans of the code, and when a caller quotes the code the warning has to be taken seriously. This time, however, there was no call, though the IRA later claimed that it had phoned the Samaritans.

That night Colin and Wendy Parry sit with their son in hospital. He is swathed in bandages and linked to a life-support machine. Colin Parry said later: 'There were times I expected him to sit up and say, "Boo, fooled you, Geronimo." Anything for a laugh, that would have been typical Tim.' When it becomes clear that there is no hope for Tim, the doctors suggest that his parents should leave the room while the life-support machine is turned off. But they stay with Tim to the end.

There was no military advantage in killing two boys in a shopping centre. They were not the enemy, but the IRA's hope was that the shock effect of the bombs would prompt the British government to withdraw from Northern Ireland to prevent further terror.

Questions

Checking the facts
1. When did the Warrington bombings take place?
2. How did Tim Parry come to be killed?
3. Who else do we hear about who died that day?
4. Normally the IRA issue a warning. What appears to have happened this time?
5. According to the writer, what do terrorists hope to gain by bombings?

What kind of boy was Tim Parry?

WRITE ABOUT

- his age and physique
- his interests
- his progress at school
- things that his parents say about him.

 This is the opening of the first chapter. How effectively does it inform you about the IRA and its methods?

COMMENT UPON

- their activities over the past thirty years
- the role of the Active Service Units
- their system of giving warnings
- the way they organised the Warrington bombing.

 How does the writer manage to convey the full horror of the Warrington bombings in this extract?

DISCUSS

- the focus on particular individuals, including Tim Parry's parents
- the contrast between accounts of ordinary activities and the horror of the violence
- the description of Tim Parry's death in hospital
- the occasional use of the present tense to create a 'documentary' style.

Grammar Spelling Punctuation

Revising capital letters

Make a list of all the words in the passage which begin with a capital letter (except those which begin sentences).

- Then sort them into lists according to *why* each word begins with a capital letter. For example: 'Because it is a proper noun …'.

Writing

Write the opening section from the introductory chapter of a similar book on a controversial subject.

- For example: blood sports, or pollution or bullying. Focus on particular individuals, to show how the issue affects ordinary people.

A CHANCE IN SIX MILLION

FROM AN AUTOBIOGRAPHY
BY MARIANNE ELSLEY

SETTING THE SCENE

Marianne Elsley begins her autobiography by recalling her happy childhood in pre-war Germany. Then the Nazis extended their power and things began to change.

My parents must have known for a long time that trouble was coming, and that the conditions in Germany looked bad, but my childhood was peaceful until I was about nine years old. Then one day in 1932, at school, I was called to the Headmistress' study in the middle of the morning. I was astonished to see my parents there; they had come to fetch me home. On the way they tried to explain to me about the Nazis and that there were men in brown uniforms posted outside our house with placards telling people that we were Jews. They had both come for me, so that I should not be frightened when I came home alone and saw this. It was all very strange to me, and quite meaningless, and I remember how puzzled I was at the idea of it all, especially seeing the young men, looking rather foolish in brown uniforms and jack-boots, stationed outside our front door. I looked at them through the net curtains of our dining room, wondering if crowds would collect, but there were few passers-by in our street, and those who did come past knew us; the fact that we were Jews was not news to them. Men in brown were to become a familiar sight and a terrifying one, but at that time it seemed merely strange. That one-day demonstration marked the beginning of the more serious incidents later on, but I went back to school the next day and almost forgot about it. I got on with my work for the entrance exam to the Grammar School, and passed that without a hitch.

Up to that time Jewishness or being a Jew had meant very little to me. I knew that unlike some of my friends I had not been christened, nor did we go to Church, and I was a little envious when my best friend paraded her new white dress and new prayer-book on Easter Sunday.

And then suddenly in 1932, I was Jewish, inescapably and obviously Jewish. The innocent, calm, comfortable days were over – for ever. Instead, for me, as a child of nine or so, a worrying time started. I was anxious and became insecure. The first major shock in our immediate family was the end of my mother's career as a doctor. She was forced to give up the work she enjoyed so much and become a housewife. The end of her practice coincided with a new law which laid down that Christian girls were no longer permitted to live in households where there was a Jewish man. Poor Anna was heartbroken, and so was I, but she had to leave and find employment elsewhere.

The security of my own small world gradually began to give way. I remember my sorrow when I was not invited to the usual round of birthday parties. I was the only Jewish girl in my form and I found to my shame and discomfort that my former friends would no longer sit next to me. We were in double desks, two by two, and the girls evidently had instructions from home to avoid sitting with me. I sat on my own. In the playground they were not allowed to talk to me or play with me. I walked around on my own. Once a year in the summer, we had an excursion day, when each class with its form teacher would go into the forest near Rostock and walk and have picnics. I came to dread this day, because I knew I would be virtually on my own, and conspicuously so. The teachers, some of whom were actually old school friends of my father's, seemed unwilling or unable to do anything about it. My work suffered and school became a sorry burden.

There were also the special indignities. I was forced to salute the Nazi flag, and during the frequent singing of the new national anthem I had to stand to attention with the others, my right arm stretched out in the familiar manner. There were regular money collections for the party; sometimes we had to bring groceries for the poor of the party, and on one occasion we 'bought' nails which we hammered into a design made in the shape of a swastika.[1]

[1] *The pattern on the Nazi flag*

All this made the everyday comings and goings of life very difficult and embarrassing. Parents of my friends whom I had known all my life, crossed to the other side of the road when they saw us coming and did not acknowledge us. They were simply not allowed to, and risked their jobs and the goodwill of the authorities if they ignored these instructions. I remember one very good friend who deliberately came across the street to greet my mother and speak to her. My mother was quite shocked and afraid for her safety, and we talked about it at length at home. Most of my former friends now belonged to the Hitler Youth, a sort of military type scout movement, and their parents began to appear in brown uniforms on ceremonial days.

My teachers, too, seemed to have to toe the party line. I was a studious and conscientious child, but it was never convenient to give me good marks, and another thing that hurt my pride was that my drawings and paintings from the art class were never pinned up for exhibition like the other childrens' although I think they deserved it.

Placards were put up outside some German shops to declare that Jews were not welcome there as customers. My parents and I, poor innocents, on this occasion trooped into our usual Chemist's shop down the road to buy a roll of film and we were thunderstruck when the proprietor turned us out, shouting abuse and pointing to his placard in front of a shop full of customers. Moreover, he followed us out into the street, shouting after us and attracting a great deal of attention. My father was, of course, well known in our small town, and this was quite horrific for him. We ran home trembling and wondering what had happened to us. The next week a Nazi newspaper was pushed through our letter box. It had a report on the impudence of the Jew Josephy who dared to ignore German signs – together with a very unpleasant caricature of my father. The owner of that shop, incidentally, was the father of a girl in my class at school, with whom I had been quite friendly and I knew him well.

Questions

Checking the facts

❶ How old was Marianne when she became aware of her 'Jewishness'?
❷ How were the Nazi demonstrators dressed?
❸ What was 'the first major shock' for Marianne?
❹ What did the Nazi law have to say about Christian girls in Jewish households?
❺ Which movement did most of Marianne's Christian friends join?

What were the main changes that took place at school, which made Marianne's life unhappy?

WRITE ABOUT

- the arrangement of the classroom
- what happened in the playground and on class excursions
- the things pupils did to show respect for the Nazi party
- the ways in which the teachers responded to Marianne's work.

 How did the Nazi laws affect non-Jews?

COMMENT UPON

- what happened with Anna, the cook
- how old friends reacted in the street
- the behaviour of teachers at school
- the reactions of some shop-owners and the newspapers.

 Show how the writer succeeds in conveying the effects of the growth of Nazism on her personally as a young girl.

DISCUSS

- the way in which the narration shows Marianne gradually coming into contact with Nazism and realising what it will mean to her
- her method of selecting those details of her daily life at school which are likely to have an impact upon a young child
- accounts of her reactions to particular events
- references to her emotional reactions to what happened.

Grammar Spelling Punctuation

Revising commas

The commas have been removed from these extracts from the passage.

- Put them back in, where you think they will add clarity, and then check your results with the original writing:

  'We were in double desks two by two and the girls evidently had instructions from home to avoid sitting with me.'

  'Once a year in the summer we had an excursion day when each class with its form teacher would go into the forest near Rostock and walk and have picnics. I came to dread this day because I knew I would be virtually on my own and conspicuously so. The teachers some of whom were actually old school friends of my father's seemed unwilling or unable to do anything about it.'

Writing

Write an autobiographical piece based on your recollections of primary school.

- Try to recall a particular incident and the emotions you experienced at the time.

HIEROGLYPHS

A FACTUAL NEWSPAPER ARTICLE

Learning objectives

- to understand how information is conveyed in a clear and interesting way
- to understand how an article can successfully combine graphics and text

Discussion

- What do you know about the ancient Egyptians? In particular, what was their writing like?

SETTING THE SCENE

This article, intended for use in schools, first appeared in the education supplement of The Guardian *newspaper.*

Picture this ...

The written language of ancient Egypt was made up of many small pictures called hieroglyphs. You can learn to understand these symbols today – and write your name in 4,000-year-old script.

The ancient Egyptians used pictures instead of letters and words to read and write. Ancient Egyptian schoolchildren had to learn 700 of these picture-words before they could leave school.

Sacred carvings

In ancient Egypt pictures told stories, just as our words do today. Each picture represented a word or a sound. Together they would make names, sentences, and even stories.

But they were not just pictures. Egyptians believed that they were the 'words of the gods'. People had their names carved in the walls of tombs, believing this would help in the afterlife. The pictures are called hieroglyphs, which in Greek means 'sacred carvings'.

Hieroglyphs have been found carved in temple walls, painted on coffins and drawn on ancient paper. The Egyptians did not have books like us. They made paper from a water-plant called papyrus. Letters, stories, jokes and even washing lists have been found written on papyrus.

Most hieroglyphs read from right to left. Some read downwards and a few read from left to right, like our writing. You can find the start by looking at the animals or people on the top line – they face the side you begin from. Look out for a group of hieroglyphs in an oval. The oval is called a *cartouche*, and only a king or queen could put their name in one.

The hieroglyph trio

There are three kinds of hieroglyph. Some are words like the one which means 'writing'. This is a picture of a pen-holder and ink pots, although it can also mean 'writer'.

A second type of hieroglyph tells us which of these two meanings, 'writer' or 'writing', is correct. A picture of a man tells us it means 'writer' (Egyptian writers are called 'scribes'). A picture of a roll of papyrus placed next to the hieroglyph tells us it means 'writing'. Instead of spaces between words, Egyptian words have this type of hieroglyph at the end so that you know when a word is finished.

The third kind of hieroglyph represents sounds. The Egyptian word for 'cat' has a cat at the end – this tells us what the word means. But, before this, there are three hieroglyphs which are sounds – together they say 'meow'.

Writing your name

Use the Egyptian alphabet on page 125. Match up the sounds of the hieroglyphs with the sounds in your name.

You may find this difficult – writing in a foreign language is never easy. Some sounds, like some of our vowel sounds, did not exist in Egyptian. Use your imagination and try different sounds to get as close to your name as possible.

Drawing the hieroglyphs may not be easy but do not worry – it took the ancient Egyptians years to learn them all. They were proud of how beautiful their writing looked and how easy it was to read. Drawing squares will help. Fit each hieroglyph neatly inside a square.

Life in Egypt

The ancient Egyptians lived along the banks of the River Nile. The river flooded every year, bringing water to the fields. Most Egyptians were farmers and only a lucky few went to school.

At school pupils learned to read and write by copying out stories in hieroglyphic writing. Some of their schoolbooks still survive.

After 12 years they were ready to work as scribes, which was thought of as the best of all jobs. One phrase Egyptian schoolchildren learned was: 'Set your heart on being a scribe, that you may direct the whole earth'. Some scribes did just this – they found jobs in the royal palace.

A speedier script

Hieroglyphic writing was slow. A quicker writing system was developed. It was called hieratic, and scribes learned this too.

Hieratic was joined-up hieroglyphic writing, used for letters and everyday business. Once it had been developed, the original hieroglyphic writing system was saved for formal use in temples and tombs.

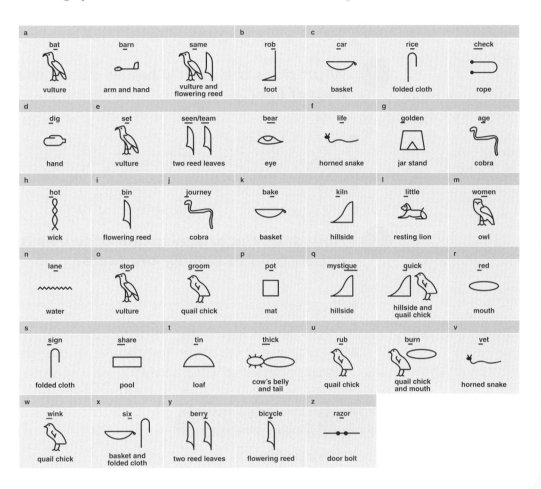

Questions

Checking the facts

❶ How many picture-words had to be learned by schoolchildren in ancient Egypt?

❷ What was their paper made from?

❸ What was the oval called which contained a king's or queen's name?

❹ What was thought to be the best job in ancient Egypt?

❺ What was the name given to joined-up hieroglyphic writing?

What are the most important facts about hieroglyphs that the article gives you in the opening sections (up to the end of the paragraph headed 'Sacred carvings')?

WRITE ABOUT

- who invented them
- where they were to be found
- how they were written
- what they looked like.

 What does the article tell us about the ancient Egyptians' way of life?

COMMENT UPON

- where the people lived
- the kinds of things that happened in school
- how and why hieroglyphs were used
- the developments that took place in the writing.

 How does the organisation of words and pictures in this article help to convey the facts?

DISCUSS

- the effectiveness of paragraphs such as 'Writing your name'
- the combination of text and drawings
- the language of the article: how successfully does the article manage to convey complex ideas simply and clearly?

Grammar Spelling Punctuation

'h' in spelling

Spelling wasn't a problem for the ancient Egyptians when they wrote a word which ends in one of the many letter-groupings containing h (such as ph, sh, ch, th, gh, rh and wh).

- Find as many examples as you can of words which begin with each of these *h* combinations.

Writing

Use an encyclopedia to find out as much as you can about the origins of the alphabet that we use to write English today.

- Then write an article similar to the one on hieroglyphs. Include illustrations to show how letters have developed. You might want to word-process your article.

THE FATE OF THE TURKEY

A NEWSPAPER ARTICLE
SETTING OUT ARGUMENTS FOR AND AGAINST

Learning objectives

- to understand how facts can be set out clearly in an article

- to understand how a piece of writing sets out arguments in a balanced way

Discussion

- What are your views on breeding animals for food? What have you heard about battery farming?

SETTING THE SCENE

This article, intended for use in schools, first appeared in the education supplement of The Guardian *newspaper.*

Bird which never misses dinner

Intensive turkey-farming has become big business but animal rights activists claim that it is cruel and unnatural.

Until 40 years ago Christmas dinner for most people in Britain was missing one element that we now think of as traditional: the high cost of turkey meant it was a luxury only better-off families could afford. But the development since the 1950s of frozen-storage facilities and household freezers has allowed the industry to supply turkeys at lower prices throughout the year.

This change, in turn, has allowed farmers to make use of turkey sheds for 12 months a year. Previously most farmers reared turkeys only in the six months leading up to Christmas. As a result, output was doubled with only a small increase in costs. Farmers could sharply reduce the price of turkey meat and still make a profit.

Other innovations in farming practice and transportation have combined to make the turkey industry even more efficient. One of the most important changes is the use of intensive farming methods, often referred to as 'factory farming'. These methods were first developed in the chicken industry after the second world war (1939–45). They are based on the principle that the largest possible quantity of meat should be produced in the quickest time, in order to keep prices low.

Until the 1950s, turkeys were commonly reared outdoors. But in recent decades they have been increasingly kept in large sheds. Farmers have found several advantages to indoor rearing. Large numbers of birds can be kept in a relatively small space. Birds also grow larger, and quicker, as they use up less energy on moving around and searching for food. They can also be gathered together more easily for slaughter.

The second big change was that farmers began to breed turkeys especially for larger size. This was done by selecting the heaviest birds and mating them with each other. This resulted in larger and heavier birds which produced more meat. Today, the average turkey produces twice as much meat as in the 1950s.

Without these developments, thousands of people would have been unable to afford to eat turkey. The rearing of greater numbers of heavier turkeys has led to a dramatic fall in today's prices. At the end of 1991, free-range turkey cost about 90p per kilogram and turkey reared in pole barns about 77p per kg, but birds reared in larger, more intensive sheds cost only about 45p per kg.

Animal rights groups say there has been a high price to pay for cheaper food: in suffering. They say that turkeys, in common with many other farm animals, are kept in unnatural conditions which cause them considerable stress and pain.

Chickens' Lib, a group campaigning against intensive poultry-farming, says that turkeys grow so quickly today that they suffer from a range of physical ailments. Many are unable to walk properly because their legs cannot support their body weight, which in older birds can reach as much as 36kg. Common problems are deformed or fractured bones, slipped tendons, arthritis and foot ulcers.

According to Chickens' Lib, turkeys are very active birds which naturally like to forage for food in the undergrowth. In confined spaces they quickly become frustrated and can become violent towards each other. At worst, they peck at each others' eyes and feet and can kill.

To prevent these attacks, many farmers use a hot blade to remove a section of the upper beaks of young birds when they are a few days old. They may also blunt the tip of the lower beak. Animal rights campaigners say this process of 'debeaking' is cruel and that it causes prolonged pain.

Most turkey farmers breed turkeys through a process known as artificial insemination. Sperm is removed from the male and then introduced into females through a tube. Alastair Mews, head of the RSPCA's farm animals department, says this is because male turkeys grow so large that females

Turkey-rearing

Free-range
Very few turkeys, maybe only 100,000 of the 11 million eaten at Christmas, are reared by 'free-range' methods. This means that birds are allowed to run freely on grass fields or woodlands.

Pole barns
About 2 million birds eaten at Christmas are reared in 'pole barns'. These are open-sided sheds with wooden planks up to about shoulder height and netting at the top. This prevents the birds from escaping and allows in light and air. Pole barns provide most of the 'farm-fresh' birds eaten at Christmas.

cannot support their weight during mating. 'People are breeding monsters which can no longer even reproduced naturally,' Mr Mews says.

But turkey farmers deny that their rearing methods are unnatural or cruel. Derek Kelly, chairman of the turkey committee of the National Farmers Union and a turkey farmer himself, says that artificial insemination is used to ensure that as many females as possible lay eggs.

Turkeys tend to peck each other when confined because 'that's the law of nature', Mr Kelly says. 'In nature, weaklings are always picked on, and that is why we trim birds' beaks – to protect them.' Mr Kelly accepts that heavier birds do have problems with their legs, but he denies that this is cruel. 'If a human limps, that's unfortunate – but is it cruel? Turkeys are like humans: you get some who can walk better than others.'

Turkey-farming is regulated by a government code of practice. The Ministry of Agriculture says it sends vets to inspect farms. If farmers are causing 'unnecessary pain or distress' to their animals, they can be prosecuted. The National Farmers Union says this ensures that turkey farming is not cruel to animals. But Chickens' Lib argues that farmers are very rarely prosecuted. The Ministry of Agriculture has prosecuted poultry farmers only three times in the past 15 years.

Windowless sheds
Most turkeys eaten during the festive season (as many as 9 million) are reared in windowless sheds. These resemble the enclosed barns which are used to rear broiler chickens. They are said to have a 'controlled environment' because there is no natural lighting and artificial fans regulate ventilation and temperature. Large sheds may hold 15,000 birds, which have less space than those in pole barns. Government veterinary investigation centres report that starvation, lack of water and heat stress are problems among birds reared for Christmas.

Questions

Checking the facts

❶ Why did most people not eat turkey for Christmas dinner forty years ago?

❷ Which technological developments in the 1950s permitted large-scale rearing of turkeys?

❸ What is the main purpose of intensive farming?

❹ What is the main argument of animal rights groups against intensive farming?

❺ Why do some farmers 'debeak' their turkeys?

A *What has been done since the 1950s to make turkeys more available and more popular for the consumer?*

WRITE ABOUT

- developments in technology in the 1950s
- intensive farming methods
- breeding turkeys for larger size.

 B *According to this extract, what are the main arguments against intensive farming?*

COMMENT UPON

- physical ailments
- confinement
- debeaking
- breeding for size and weight.

 C *How balanced is this article? Is it even-handed, or does it favour one side of the argument over the other?*

DISCUSS

- the way in which the background to the debate is established
- how the arguments for and against intensive farming are presented
- the facts selected for the concluding paragraph
- the use of the three photographs and the information set out in the captions.

Grammar Spelling Punctuation

Clauses

Each of the following sentences contains a main and a subordinate clause.

- Which is the main clause in each case, A or B?

  (A) I enjoy turkey at Christmas, (B) although it gives me indigestion.

  (A) My sister doesn't eat it (B) because she's a vegetarian.

  (A) If turkeys are kept indoors, (B) farmers can rear them in large numbers.

  (A) Before frozen storage was developed (B) not many people could afford turkey.

  (A) Turkeys can suffer (B) when they grow so quickly.

Writing

Write a newspaper article on a subject about which you feel strongly.

- You might want to try to maintain a balance between the two sides of the argument, or simply put forward points to support one side. Research the facts thoroughly before you begin to plan your article.

NURSING IN THE GREAT WAR

FROM A LETTER BY ELEONORA B PEMBERTON

Learning objectives

- to understand how a writer's own personality can be seen in a letter

- to understand how letter-writers have their own styles

Discussion

- Discuss what you know about the combat conditions of the Great War. You might have learned some of the details from the poems of Wilfred Owen, history lessons at school, or even *Blackadder Goes Fourth*.

SETTING THE SCENE

Eleonora B Pemberton was serving as a volunteer nurse in France when she wrote this letter to her mother in 1914. Here she is writing about some of the British soldiers ('Tommies') in the hospital.

The longer I am here, the more sorry I am for the poor Tommies' home people. Officers have so many more means of communicating with them and setting their minds at rest; they can tip orderlies to telegraph for them – often their wives can come out or friends are asked to look them up; but Tommy is just one of the herd; he has neither pens, ink nor paper, even if he feels well enough to write and as many of them have said when I have asked them – 'I'm not much good at writing, Sister – *you* write for me'. In most cases they had hardly anything in the way of *news* to suggest and yet when one persevered one could drag quite an interesting story of personal exploits out of them. One Scotch boy commissioned me to write to his sweetheart, a barmaid at Lyndhurst, and was prepared to say nothing except that he was wounded and hoped she would write. A little probing, however, elicited details which would interest her immensely. He said that he was attached to the cyclist corps of (I think, but I muddle them up rather!) the Scots Guards. At 1 am they received the order to advance upon a certain German position: it was pitch dark as they pedalled rapidly along, eyes & ears alert for an alarm which might mean their last moment. Arrived within 20 *yards* of the

Germans, they left their machines by the road side and crawled with fixed bayonets nearer and nearer until suddenly, the word 'charge' was given & they were there, right on top of the Germans thrusting and stabbing in the dark at a foe they could only see when a gun was fired. It was a weird sensation, he said, but for him it did not last long as he was shot at close range by the friend of a man into whom he had just stuck his bayonet, and after that he knew no more. He was very bad and in great pain when he first came into hospital but now he is better.

When I was up at the Casino the other day the Sister showed me a case of Tetanus, the only one they had. He was not *very* bad & they had some hopes of him recovering. Sir Almroth Wright is here and he had injected the anti-toxin and the man's leg had been opened right up and gauze kept wet with sea water threaded through it and fresh sea water was constantly being added. Isn't that interesting. I must try and go and hear how it succeeds.

A few nights ago we had come back from the station and started dinner when a message came from the Quartermaster that Preston – who drives our motor ambulance – and I were to go off at once to an outlying station to fetch three men with fever and take them to any hospital wh. could find room for them. Off we went in the dark, hunted up the R.T.O. office (wh. had been moved since I had last been there) and were told that the train was just coming in. It contained those of the British troops from India who had not been well enough to go up to the front with the rest of their regiments. They had been in hospital at Havre or Rouen or somewhere & were now going up, but these three had developed fever and were to be again left. We waited in our 'bus' having got it as comfortable as possible & presently three chattering ague-stricken wretches were delivered over to us, and Preston & I started off with them.

An armoured train is lying in a siding close to us, painted in dabs every colour of the rainbow. The German shells are similarly painted and it is said that the colours fade into the background & look like trees!

Heaps of love to Dad & your little self from your loving Nora.

Questions

Checking the facts

❶ Why does the writer feel sorry for the Tommies?

❷ Who shot the 'Scotch boy'?

❸ How were they treating the man with tetanus?

❹ Why did the writer have to meet three soldiers off the train?

A *Describe how the 'Scotch boy' came to be wounded.*

WRITE ABOUT

- the corps to which he was attached
- their means of attack
- how the boy himself came to be wounded.

B *What do we learn from this letter about the writer?*

COMMENT UPON

- her attitude towards the Tommies
- her interest in medical matters
- the matter-of-fact way in which she deals with dramatic stories.

C *What is interesting about the writer's style?*

DISCUSS

- the sometimes informal and colloquial language
- her avoidance of 'dramatic' language
- her use of 'chatty' asides in parenthesis (brackets), and abbreviations.

Grammar Spelling Punctuation

Wh- clauses

One of Eleonora B Pemberton's abbreviations is *wh.* for *which*, as in the sentence '...and take them to any hospital wh. could find room for them.' The *which clause* allows her to give more detail about the hospital.

- Match up the (slightly abbreviated) main clauses on the left with the correct *which* ... and *who* ... clause on the right. The examples are to be found in the passage:

Off we went in the dark, hunted up the RTO office	who had not been well enough to go up to the front ...
It contained those of the British troops from India	(which had been moved since I had last been there) ...

Writing

Think of other occasions in history when people wrote letters home describing what they were doing.

- Write a letter like Eleonora B Pemberton's. Think first about the period of history in which you are writing and about the person who will be receiving your letter. How will the character of the writer be revealed in what they write? You could try to imitate the language of the period or simply write in modern English.

COMICS AND SCIENCE

A NEWSPAPER FEATURE ARTICLE

Learning objectives

- to understand how information is conveyed in a clear and interesting way
- to understand how an argument can be developed in a newspaper article

Discussion

- Discuss science fiction comics that you have read. What picture do they give of science and scientific developments?

SETTING THE SCENE

This article, intended for use in schools, first appeared in the education supplement of The Guardian *newspaper.*

For more than a century children and adults alike have lived out the fantastic adventures of characters such as Colonel Dan Dare and the Incredible Hulk through the medium of comics. As the comic-book artists prepare to take their colourful creations into the next millennium, we look at how scientists have been represented in drawings and how the image of science itself has changed over the years.

In the last three decades there has been an interesting shift in public attitudes towards science. Scientists, once considered the group of people who could herald a new age of technology and improved living standards, are now often regarded with more mistrust as the source of what is *wrong* in our environment. You can see this change clearly in the medium of comics.

In the early 1950s, a positive attitude towards science – a belief in its power to bring good – could be seen very clearly in comic books, which provided an outlet for the imagination of child and adult alike.

Many children who grew up during the 1950s and 60s waited with bated breath each week for the next copy of the *Eagle* so that they could follow the adventures of Colonel Daniel McGregor Dare, better known to his fans as Dan Dare.

Dan Dare was born and educated in Manchester and eventually graduated as Bachelor of Astro-Physics at London University. His father was chief test pilot for Cosmic Spaceships. Dan became chief pilot for the 'Space Fleet' at the age of 26.

Dan was a well-known 'goodie' – on many occasions it was evident that his worthy exploits were only possible because of the application of his scientific knowledge. For example, Dan thwarted the mining of plutonium for use in weapons.

It was also Dan who revealed that a new chemical, 'tungstal-maximite spray', was being used to protect the Big Ben clock-tower from weathering. The character was not concerned that industrial pollution had caused the weathering; the important thing was that *science* had found an answer.

This reflected the hope many people had of science as the source of answers to all human problems, and not as the source of those problems themselves.

It was a similar story for the contemporaries of Dan Dare in comics such as *Lion* and *Tiger*. Jet Ace Logan usually managed to conquer the aliens by the application of science.

One such incident required the use of instant photographs to expose aliens who could take on any form. This story was written long before Polaroid cameras had been developed.

But the fear that science can be a double-edged sword, having the potential for both good and evil, has been around for many years. The story of Dr Jekyll and Mr Hyde, first published in 1886 – which has also appeared in comic form since then – tells the tale of a doctor obsessed with the thought of producing a drug that could separate the good and evil sides of someone's personality. The result, predictably, is that it sent him mad: a very clear warning about the dangers of uncontrolled science.

An idea similar to this was developed years later in comics, and then on television. Dr David Banner, a scientist, tried to isolate the inner strength that people have in a time of crisis. He tried the use of radiation to achieve this end but predictably his work went wrong. The Incredible Hulk was born.

Over the years a group of 'super-heroes', such as the Incredible Hulk, has developed. The heroes have usually gained extraordinary powers as the result of some terrible accident in a scientific experiment. These include Mighty Atom and Spider-Man among others.

But of the modern comic-book 'super-heroes' the only one that has achieved his powers by the *application* of science and technology is

Batman. Even then, his arch-enemy, the Joker, is a the result of a chemical accident. He fell into a large vat of chemicals which made him hideously ugly and forced him to disguise himself with make-up. Corrosive Man, who burned his way through Gotham City, was another chemical horror, this time created from toxic waste. More recently we have had radioactive accidents giving us Teenage Mutant Hero Turtles.

In the 1950s and early 60s the vision of the scientist as seen in comics was one who would create wonders and solve problems.

Many of the comics actually included straight factual pieces about scientific principles. For example, in the *Eagle Annual* there was old Professor Brittain explaining all about electricity. Some comics also had sections explaining the rudiments of atomic energy. But events which appear to have left science with a bad image, such as chemical and nuclear disasters, have led to changes in the way scientists have been portrayed by comics and other media.

Examples of such horrifying disasters include the gas leak at Bhopal in India in 1984 when thousands of people died and the fire at the Chernobyl nuclear reactor in what was the Soviet Union in 1986.

Heroes or baddies?
As the medium of comics moved into the 1970s and 1980s, there was a significant shift away from scientists as heroic figures who would provide the public with a better tomorrow. Today the dominant heroes will try to make the best of the mess the scientist has created by trying to repair damage caused to the environment such as at Bhopal and Chernobyl, for example.

This has meant, typically, that the physical or chemical horror taking place leaves the world either with a 'super-hero' or 'super-baddie'. Either way, it is the image of science itself that is being criticised.

Questions

Checking the facts
❶ Which popular 1950s comic featured Dan Dare?
❷ Which story published in 1886 told of a doctor obsessed with the idea of separating the good and evil sides of someone's personality?
❸ What image did comics in the 1950s and 1960s give of science and scientists?
❹ What in particular happened in the 1980s which helped to change the ways in which science and scientists were portrayed in comics?

A *What do you learn from the article about the comic characters Dan Dare and Jet Ace Logan?*

WRITE ABOUT

- when they appeared in comics
- Dan Dare's background and education
- the ways in which Dan Dare was a 'goodie'
- the examples given of Dan Dare's and Jet Ace Logan's uses of science
- the ways in which ideas from the comics might have helped science at that time.

 B *How have the bad effects of science been represented in literature, comics and other media?*

COMMENT UPON

- one of the earliest stories, published in 1886
- a similar idea later developed in comics and on television
- Batman and his enemies
- changes in comics in the 1970s and 1980s.

 C *What does the article say about the changes in the representation of science and scientists?*

DISCUSS

- the ways in which people's attitudes towards science and scientists are depicted
- the use of particular examples of positive and negative images of science and scientists
- the references to events in the real world
- the introduction and conclusion to the article.

Grammar Spelling Punctuation

Brackets & dashes

Brackets and dashes are used for parenthesis: when we want to show the reader that we are marking off a piece of extra information in a sentence. Dashes usually have a stronger effect, making the added material stand out more.

- In pairs, find examples in this unit and others of brackets and dashes used for parenthesis. Discuss whether the words placed in dashes seem to stand out more than those placed in brackets.

Writing

Write a review of a comic or graphic novel which particularly interests you.

- It might be one that you remember from your childhood, or something you have read recently. Pick out its main features and try to say what it is that has made it popular.

137

LETTER TO DANIEL

AN AUTOBIOGRAPHY IN THE FORM OF A <u>LETTER</u>

Learning objectives

- to understand how facts are conveyed in autobiography

- to understand how a writer expresses deep-felt emotions through the medium of an imagined letter

Discussion

- What kind of life do BBC foreign correspondents lead? Which parts of the world might they have been sent to in recent years and what would they have experienced there?

SETTING THE SCENE

Fergal Keane is a BBC correspondent who has worked all over the world. 'Letter to Daniel' was written just after the birth of his son.

[1] *Daniel Patrick Keane was born on 4 February, 1996.*

Hong Kong, February 1996 [1]

My dear son, it is six o'clock in the morning on the island of Hong Kong. You are asleep cradled in my left arm and I am learning the art of one-handed typing. Your mother, more tired yet more happy that I've ever known her, is sound asleep in the room next door and there is soft quiet in our apartment.

When you're older we'll tell you that you were born in Britain's last Asian colony in the lunar year of the pig and that when we brought you home, the staff of our apartment block gathered to wish you well. 'It's a boy, so lucky, so lucky. We Chinese love boys,' they told us. One man said you were the first baby to be born in the block in the year of the pig. This, he told us, was good Feng Shui, in other words a positive sign for the building and everyone who lived there.

Naturally your mother and I were only too happy to believe that. We wanted you and waited for you, imagined you and dreamed about you and now that you are here no dream can do justice to you.

We have called you Daniel Patrick but I've been told by my Chinese friends that you should have a Chinese name as well and this glorious dawn sky makes me think we'll call you Son of the Eastern Star.

Like many foreign correspondents I know, I have lived a life that, on occasion, has veered close to the edge: war zones, natural disasters, darkness in all its shapes and forms.

In a world of insecurity and ambition and ego, it's easy to be drawn in, to take chances with our lives, to believe that what we do and what people say about us is reason enough to gamble with death. Now, looking at your sleeping face, inches away from me, listening to your occasional sigh and gurgle, I wonder how I could have ever thought glory and prizes and praise were sweeter than life.

And it's also true that I am pained, perhaps haunted is a better word, by the memory, suddenly so vivid now, of each suffering child I have come across on my journeys. To tell you the truth, it's nearly too much to bear at this moment to even think of children being hurt and abused and killed. And yet looking at you, the images come flooding back. Ten-year-old Andi Mikail dying from napalm burns on a hillside in Eritrea, how his voice cried out, growing ever more faint when the wind blew dust on to his wounds. The two brothers, Domingo and Juste, in Menongue, southern Angola. Juste, two years old and blind, dying from malnutrition, being carried on seven-year-old Domingo's back. And Domingo's words to me, 'He was nice before, but now he has the hunger.'

Last October, in Afghanistan, when you were growing inside your mother, I met Sharja, aged twelve. Motherless, fatherless, guiding me through the grey ruins of her home, everything was gone, she told me. And I knew that, for all her tender years, she had learned more about loss than I would likely understand in a lifetime.

There is one last memory. Of Rwanda, and the churchyard of the parish of Nyarabuye where, in a ransacked classroom, I found a mother and her three young children huddled together where they'd been beaten to death. The children had died holding on to their mother, that instinct we all learn from birth and in one way or another cling to until we die.

Daniel, these memories explain some of the fierce protectiveness I feel for you, the tenderness and the occasional moments of blind terror when I imagine anything happening to you. But there is something more, a story from long ago that I will tell you face to face, father to son, when you are older. It's a very personal story but it's part of the picture. It has to do with the long lines of blood and family, about our lives and how we can get lost in them and, if we're lucky, find our way out again into the sunlight.

It begins thirty-five years ago in a big city on a January morning with snow on the ground and a woman walking to hospital to have her first baby. She is in her early twenties and the city is still strange to her, bigger and noisier than the easy streets and gentle hills of her distant home. She's walking because there is no money and everything of value has been pawned to pay for the alcohol to which her husband has become addicted.

On the way, a taxi driver notices her sitting, exhausted and cold, in the doorway of a shop and he takes her to hospital for free. Later that day, she gives birth to a baby boy and, just as you are to me, he is the best thing she has ever seen. Her husband comes that night and weeps with joy when he sees his son. He is truly happy. Hungover, broke, but in his own way happy, for they were both young and in love with each other and their son.

But, Daniel, time had some bad surprises in store for them. The cancer of alcoholism ate away at the man and he lost his family. This was not something he meant to do or wanted to do, it just was. When you are older, my son, you will learn about how complicated life becomes, how we can lose our way and how people get hurt inside and out. By the time his son had grown up, the man lived away from his family, on his own in a one-roomed flat, living and dying for the bottle.

He died on the fifth of January, one day before the anniversary of his son's birth, all those years before in that snowbound city. But his son was too far away to hear his last words, his final breath, and all the things they might have wished to say to one another were left unspoken.

Yet now, Daniel, I must tell you that when you let out your first powerful cry in the delivery room of the Adventist Hospital and I became a father, I thought of your grandfather and, foolish though it may seem, hoped that in some way he could hear, across the infinity between the living and the dead, your proud statement of arrival. For if he could hear, he would recognise the distinct voice of family, the sound of hope and new beginnings that you and all your innocence and freshness have brought to the world.

Questions

Checking the facts

❶ When and where was Daniel born?

❷ What do Fergal Keane's Chinese friends think about the birth?

❸ Name three of the countries about which he has recent memories.

❹ How old is Fergal Keane himself?

❺ Why did his own mother have no money when he was born?

What do we learn about the birth of Fergal Keane's son?

WRITE ABOUT

- the country in which he was born
- the year of his birth, as the Chinese describe it
- the reactions of the Chinese staff in the apartment block
- the name he has been given and the additional Chinese name that he might have.

 What range of emotions have been stirred by the birth of his son and how are they conveyed?

COMMENT UPON

- the account of his and his wife's reactions to the birth
- the ways in which the birth has changed his attitude to ambition and the risks that he has taken
- his feelings about the children encountered on recent assignments.

 How does Fergal Keane manage to link the feelings he has for his new son with his feelings for his dead father?

DISCUSS

- Keane's feelings of protectiveness towards his son
- the story Keane tells of his own birth, and his reasons for telling it
- the sympathetic account of his father's alcoholism and death
- Keane's hopes, concerning his father, when Daniel was born.

Grammar Spelling Punctuation

Paragraphs

A paragraph is a way of organising ideas in a long piece of writing.

- Which paragraph in the letter has only one sentence, and which paragraph contains most sentences?

- Write a 'topic heading' for each paragraph in the letter. For example, the first two might be: 'Setting the scene' and 'Getting used to having a baby'.

Writing

Write a letter to someone about a moment in your life which made a great impression on you.

- You might address it to a close friend or relative; and you could base it upon a real or imagined event.

THE GREAT FIRE OF LONDON

A DIARY ENTRY BY AN EYE-WITNESS, SAMUEL PEPYS

Learning objectives

- to understand how a diary-writer records dramatic and impressive events
- to understand how good diary writing can be personal, detailed and vivid

Discussion

- Why do people keep diaries? What kinds of things make diaries from the past really interesting to read?

SETTING THE SCENE

Samuel Pepys is probably the most famous diarist ever to have written in the English language. He lived in the seventeenth century and wrote this entry for September 2nd, 1666.

Some of our maids sitting up late last night to get things ready against our feast to-day, Jane called us up about three in the morning, to tell us of a great fire they saw in the City. So I rose, and slipped on my night-gown, and went to her window; and thought it to be on the back-side of Marke-lane at the farthest; but, being unused to such fires as followed, I thought it far enough off; and so went to bed again, and to sleep. About seven rose again to dress myself, and there looked out at the window, and saw the fire not so much as it was, and further off. So to my closet to set things to rights, after yesterday's cleaning. By and by Jane comes and tells me that she hears that above 300 houses have been burned down to-night by the fire we saw, and that it is now burning down all Fish Street, by London Bridge. So I made myself ready presently, and walked to the Tower; and there got up upon one of the high places, Sir J. Robinson's little son going up with me; and there I did see the houses at that end of the bridge all on fire, and an infinite great fire on this and the other side the end of the bridge; which, among other people, did trouble me for poor little Michell and our Sarah on the bridge. So down, with my heart full of trouble, to the Lieutenant of the Tower, who tells me that it begun this morning in the King's baker's house in Pudding-lane, and that it hath burned down St Magnus's Church and most part of Fish Street already. So I down to the water-side, and there got a boat, and through bridge, and there saw a lamentable fire. Poor Michell's house, as far as the Old Swan, already burned that way, and the fire running further, that, in a very little time, it got as far as the Steele-yard, while I was there. Every body endeavouring to remove their goods, and flinging into the river, or bringing them into lighters that lay off; poor people staying in their houses as long as till the very fire touched them, and then running into boats, or clambering from one pair of stairs, by the waterside, to another. And, among other things, the poor pigeons, I perceive, were loth to leave their houses, but hovered about the windows and balconys, till they burned their wings, and fell down.

At last met my Lord Mayor in Canning Street, like a man spent, with a handkercher about his neck. Like a fainting woman, he cried, 'Lord! what can I do? I am spent: people will not obey me. I have been pulling down houses; but the fire overtakes us faster than we can do it.' That he needed no more soldiers; and that, for himself, he must go and refresh himself, having been up all night. So he left me, and I him, and walked home; seeing people all almost distracted, and no manner of means used to quench the fire. The houses, too, so very thick thereabouts, and full of matter for burning, as pitch and tar, in Thames Street; and warehouses of oyle, and wines, and brandy, and other things. Here I saw Mr Isaac Houblon, the handsome man, prettily dressed and dirty at his door at Dowgate, receiving some of his brother's things, whose houses were on fire; and, as he says, have been removed twice already; and he doubts, as it soon proved, that they must be, in a little time, removed from his house also, which was a sad consideration. And to see the churches all filling with goods by people who themselves should have been quietly there at this time.

I also did see a poor cat taken out of a hole in a chimney, joyning to the wall of the Exchange, with the hair all burnt off the body, and yet alive.

Questions

Checking the facts

❶ How many houses were burned down during the first night?
❷ Which areas of London did Pepys see burning from his viewpoint on the Tower?
❸ Where did he then go for a better view?
❹ Where did the fire begin?
❺ Why has the Lord Mayor been pulling down houses?

143

Which sights and events seem to have impressed Pepys most?

WRITE ABOUT

- his first views of the fire
- his visit to the Tower
- what he saw from the river
- what was happening in the churches.

 Show how Pepys manages to convey the dramatic impact the fire is having.

COMMENT UPON

- his references to individuals by name and his comments on how they are being affected
- his observations on the effect the fire is having on the population of London more generally
- his references to animals.

 What are the major features of Pepys's diary writing?

DISCUSS

- his use of details of everyday life
- the way he focuses on the fates of individuals as well as people he does not know personally
- his ability to enable us to 'see' the scenes he describes.

Grammar Spelling Punctuation

The changing language: meanings & spellings

Which words would we use today instead of the following?

against (line 1, p.142)   presently (line 12, p.142)   hath (line 2, p.143)
handkercher (line 15, p.143)   prettily (line 24, p.143)   doubts (line 27, p.143)

Writing

Write two or three diary entries by an eye-witness to a dramatic event in history.

- Decide whether you are going to be a participator in the event, or merely someone looking on. Think about a dramatic happening which lasted at least two or three days.